George L. Thomas

THE CASE OF THERESE NEUMANN

The Case of

Therese Neumann

by

HILDA C. GRAEF

The Newman Press · Westminster, Maryland

1951

Nihil Obstat: HENRICUS F. DAVIS, M.A., S.T.D.
Censor Deputatus.

Imprimatur: ✠ JOSEPH
Archiepiscopus Birmingamiensis.
Birmingamiae, 30a Aprilis 1950.

Contents

Preface

WHEN I undertook to write a book on Therese Neumann I was not aware of the complications of the subject, which became apparent only in the course of my studies; so that I began to wonder whether I ought to write on it at all. In this difficulty I was unexpectedly given the opportunity to discuss the matter with several theologians of mark, and these conversations encouraged me to go on with the work.

It may perhaps be useful to indicate the principal sources frequently cited in the following pages, since many of them will be unknown to the average English reader. 1. For the history and interpretation of Therese Neumann's illnesses and cures I base myself chiefly on the book of Dr. B. de Poray-Madeyski, *Le cas de la visionnaire stigmatisée Thérèse Neumann de Konnersreuth*, Paris 1940. The work bears the Imprimatur *Ex Vicariato Urbis*, and the concluding sentence of the author's introduction, " Bien qu'honoré de l'approbation des Supérieures Autorités ecclésiastiques, nous n'entendons en aucune façon en tirer argument en faveur de notre thèse . . ." implies that it is held in high esteem in official quarters. 2. The *Études Carmélitaines* is generally considered one of the most reliable and best-informed periodicals on questions of mystical and ascetical theology. We cite from it authors of such international reputation as Abbé Charles Journet, Professor at the Grand Séminaire of Fribourg (to whom my particular thanks are due for much valuable personal help and advice), the late Dom Alois Mager, O.S.B., Professor at the Catholic University of Salzburg and author of several learned works on the Psychology of Mysticism; the Carmelite

Père Bruno de Jésus-Marie, biographer of St. John of the Cross, and several others. 3. We have also consulted the two volumes of Dr. Gerlich (his degree is not medical but literary), a Calvinist from East Prussia who later became an editor of a Munich newspaper and an ardent admirer and convert of Therese. Despite his exertions the German edition of his book on her did not receive the Imprimatur. 4. Unfortunately I had no access to the biography of Leopold Witt (cited therefore only from secondary sources), who was parish priest of the Bavarian village of Muenchenreuth from 1920 to 1931; the first edition of his book entitled *Die Leiden einer Gluecklichen* (The Sufferings of a Happy Woman) did not receive the Imprimatur. 5. Teodorowicz, on whose work *Mystical Phenomena in the Life of Theresa Neumann* we rely for most of our descriptions of her spiritual experiences, was Archbishop of Lemberg; his work has been criticized for lack of critical objectivity by Professor Jean L'hermitte and Dom Aloys Mager in the *Études Carmélitaines*, October, 1936.

6. My special gratitude is due to the Reverend Professor Dr. Michael Waldmann, who has assisted me throughout and to whose generosity I owe all the hitherto unpublished material in this book. Professor Waldmann, after being Professor of Moral Theology at Dillingen, has held the same chair at Regensburg where he is still lecturing especially on mystical theology and parapsychology; he has contributed important articles on Stigmatization, Parapsychology and similar subjects to the standard German Catholic Dictionary *Lexicon fuer Theologie und Kirche*. He attended the seminary together with Therese Neumann's director, Fr. Naber, and has followed the events of Konnersreuth from 1926 onwards. I owe the introduction to him to the Vicar General of the Regensburg diocese.

After thanking him and Abbé Journet, may I also use this opportunity to say how much I owe to those priests and laymen who, by listening patiently to my arguments, have helped me considerably to clarify my mind on this controversial subject. Last, but by no means least, I wish to express my gratitude to the Mercier Press* and to its literary staff, who have given me every help by procuring necessary literature, facilitating my journey to Konnersreuth, and making most valuable suggestions concerning the manuscript.

H. C. GRAEF.

Oxford,
   Feast of the Transfiguration
   of Our Lord, 1949.

* The Mercier Press, of Cork, Ireland, is the original publisher of *The Case of Therese Neumann.*

Introduction

THE SUBJECT of the present study, the stigmatized Bavarian, Therese Neumann of Konnersreuth, has caused much controversy, not only between Catholics and Protestants, but also among Catholics themselves, whether theologians, doctors or laymen. If, then, we undertake to add yet another work to the already voluminous literature on Konnersreuth, it is with the desire to contribute as balanced and impartial an account of the facts as possible, our sources being personal observation and already published material, much of which has not yet appeared in English.

The guiding principles for this study are taken from the writings of the mystical Doctor of the Church, St. John of the Cross, whose pronounced reserve in regard to all extraordinary phenomena, apparitions, visions and the like will constantly be kept in view. "I say, then," he writes, "that with regard to all those imaginary visions and apprehensions and to all other forms and species whatsoever, which present themselves beneath some particular kind of knowledge or image or form, whether they be false and come from the devil or are recognized as true and coming from God, the understanding must not be embarrassed by them or feed upon them."[1] And we trust we shall not misinterpret the great doctor if we apply his words not only to the recipients of these visions, but also to those who hear and recount them.

In times of great emotional stress, after wars and revolutions, there is often a hunger for the extraordinary, the "supernatural," the term here understood in its popular, not in its theological sense. The story of Therese Neumann ran like wild fire through Germany and beyond after the Great War of 1914–1918, and it has flared up again after the defeat of

[1] *Complete Works*, Westminster, Md., 1946, I, p. 132.

Hitler, during the occupation of Bavaria by the American Army. It is truly an extraordinary story, and the human mind is only too much inclined to be attracted by the extraordinary. It tends to go after the things that "take one's breath away"; it is apt to lose or at least to suspend its critical faculties before phenomena that seem inexplicable by natural means. But it is not extraordinary phenomena that nourish the life of the soul. God will, from time to time, produce them to recall men to the love of their Maker; or, if they be not directly produced by Him, but are due to abnormal human factors or even to diabolical interference, will permit them and draw good out of them. Yet it can be dangerous to allow them too great an influence on the spiritual life. The one sure and infallible means of union between God and the soul is dark faith, as St. John never wearies of telling his readers. And it was a greater one than St. John of the Cross who said: "Blessed are they that have not seen and have believed." If Our Lord said that to St. Thomas after He had shown him His own glorious Wounds, how much more applicable are these words where stigmatization is concerned. The stigmatist may show forth the Wounds of Christ in the body, yet Our Lord Himself commends those whose faith needs no such signs. He Himself performed miracles; yet He did not command men to learn from Him how to raise the dead or to multiply loaves. He commanded them to learn something very different: "Learn from me, for I am meek and humble of heart."

The Church has heeded His teaching and has always made humility the touchstone of sanctity. Thus, in dealing with the happenings at Konnersreuth, we shall from time to time apply this test. Visions, ecstasies, stigmata and other phenomena appear indeed glorious to the eyes of men; but God judges by different standards, standards which have been revealed by Our Lord. In the following study the attempt will be made to examine the case of Therese Neumann in the light of the teaching of Scripture and of the Doctors and Saints of the Church, without undue emphasis on the many strange phenomena, bearing in mind the advice of the great Apostle, to "be zealous for the better gifts."

On Stigmatization

STIGMATIZATION belongs to the kind of graces that theologians call *gratiae gratis datae*, which means that they are not necessary for sanctity but are given by the bounty of God for the edification of others rather than for the sanctification of the recipient. Whereas sanctifying grace (*gratia gratum faciens*) cannot be observed by the senses—the effects of Baptism or of sacramental confession are invisible—the *gratiae gratis datae*, such as miracles, stigmata, levitation and the like, can be seen or heard or touched and are, for this reason, despite the warnings of theologians, often more highly esteemed than the invisible sanctifying grace. For what can be perceived by the senses will always make a greater appeal to the majority of men than the hidden things that can be apprehended only by faith.

For this reason attachment to such graces is dangerous. As St. John of the Cross says: " These supernatural works and graces may be practised by those who are not in a state of grace and charity," [2] and continues: " Three principal evils, it seems to me, may come to the soul when it sets its rejoicing upon supernatural good. These are: that it may deceive and be deceived; that it may fall away from faith; and that it may indulge in vainglory or some other such vanity. As to the first of these, it is a very easy thing to deceive others, and to deceive oneself, by rejoicing in this kind of operation. And the reason is that, in order to know which of these works are false and which are true, and how and at what time they should be practised, much counsel and much light from God are needful, and both these are greatly impeded by joy in these operations and esteem for them. And for two reasons: first, because joy

[2] *Ibid.*, p. 300.

deadens and darkens judgment; second, because, when a man has joy in these things, not only does he the more quickly become eager to obtain them, but he is also the more impelled to work them out of the proper season." [3]

Stigmatization, then, and features that frequently accompany it such as visions, prophetic gifts, hierognosis, etc., have to be treated with as much reserve as other *gratiae gratis datae,* since there may be present the danger of deception or illusion. For the fact must be kept in mind that there are not only stigmata of demonic origin, which imitate the stigmata of the saints in all external characteristics,[4] but also, as has been discovered in recent times, those of purely natural origin, connected especially with hysteria. Hence it is necessary to judge such phenomena by the signs of sanctity required by the Church before it is possible to assume that the wounds are divinely bestowed.

The problem is of little importance if, as in the case of a St. Francis, St. Catherine of Siena, or St. Gemma Galgani, the person who receives the stigmata is already far advanced in sanctity. After the profound purifications of the " Night of the Spirit " demonic deception is so improbable that it may be safely ruled out. "If there is infused contemplation," writes Dom Aloys Mager, "one can have no doubt about the origin of the stigmata." [5] For even should there be an hysterical foundation—a possibility that ought always to be kept in mind—the Holy Ghost would have no difficulty in using this natural condition as an instrument for His own ends. In such cases, then, the only question would be whether the stigmata are, in the terminology of Journet,[6] diapsychological and diaphysiological, or parapsychological and paraphysiological. Stigmatization, according to Journet, is diapsychological if the supernatural agent utilizes psychological and physiological data, such as a particular tendency of the nervous system and especially of the

[3] *ibid.,* p. 301f.

[4] Cf. C. Journet in *Études Carmélitaines,* Oct., 1936, p. 185. All further references are to this volume unless otherwise noted.

[5] *ibid.,* p. 152.

[6] *ibid.,* pp. 180ff.

imagination, to assist in the production of the stigmata. This is
the explanation St. Francis de Sales gives of the stigmatization
of St. Francis of Assisi. The soul of the saint, when contemplating the crucified seraph, was transformed into another
crucifix, and, " as form and mistress of the body, using her
power over it, impressed the pains of the wounds by which
she was wounded in the places corresponding to those in
which her Beloved had endured them. Love is admirably
capable of sharpening the imagination, so that it can penetrate
even to the exterior." [7] Yet in the opinion of St. Francis de
Sales and his contemporaries, the imagination is not powerful
enough to produce open wounds. For that, continues the saint,
the preternatural action of the seraph is needed, being, as it
were, engrafted on the natural data.[8]

The parapsychological explanation, on the other hand—the
word is here taken in a peculiar, not in the commonly accepted,
sense of the science of parapsychology—rules out the psychological activities in the production of the stigmata and visualizes
a movement not from within to without, but from the exterior
to the interior. The stigmata of St. Francis and St. Catherine,
for example, would be explicable on this assumption, too, if the
saints' recitals of the apparitions of the seraph and of Our Lord
were taken as referring to external apparitions in the sense of
St. Thomas.[9]

If, however, a person's stigmata cannot be treated as a
mystical phenomenon within the context of the contemplative
life, they may be considered as either charismata or as natural
or preternatural phenomena. This is what Dom Mager writes
on the subject of charismatic stigmatization: " A charismatic
stigmatization would take place by an immediate intervention
of God, divorced from all natural psychogenic and normally
supernatural factors. It goes without saying that such a case
is possible, but we would not dare to affirm that it has ever
taken place. None of those known to us enters into this cate-
gory. In order to admit such a case it would have to justify

---

[7] *Traité de l'Amour de Dieu*, Bk. 6, Ch. 15.
[8] *ibid.*
[9] *Summa Theologica* III, q. 76, a.8 corp.

itself by a very important cause as regards the interests of God and the salvation of souls." [10]   For prophecy and visions God may make use of very imperfect or even sinful instruments, as, for example, in the case of Caiaphas.   But true stigmatization of its very nature involves an extraordinary physical assimilation to His Son, and one would not expect this to be produced in a person whose internal assimilation is still very imperfect. St. John of the Cross, speaking of the stigmatization of St. Francis, says: " If the effect of the (interior) wound (of love) should sometimes be permitted to show itself in the bodily senses, in a way corresponding to the interior wound, the effect of the impact and the wound will be felt without, as came to pass when the seraph wounded the soul of St. Francis with love, and in that way the effect of those wounds became outwardly visible.   For God bestows no favours upon the body without bestowing them first and principally upon the soul." [11]

If these last words be taken as they stand they not only preclude a purely charismatic stigmatization altogether, but demand for a true stigmatization the attainment of a high stage in the mystical life; for " wounds of love " are not bestowed in its beginning.   It is difficult, indeed, to see how they could be interpreted so as to fit a case of non-mystical stigmatization; and it is equally difficult to disregard them.   For the mystical Doctor is here obviously not voicing a chance opinion but enunciating a principle of the spiritual life; and a case contradicting it would have to be most clear and unequivocal in order to be admitted as an exception to the rule.

Even a case of charismatic stigmatization, however, would have to conform to certain rules.   Père Garrigou-Lagrange gives the following: " If the stigmata are charismatic, they do not necessarily presuppose consummate, or nearly consummate, sanctity.   But it is very probable that they are not bestowed on mediocre souls (*des âmes vulgaires*), still less on grossly sinful souls, hence the necessity of a moral and spiritual examination of the person.   It must be ascertained, not only

[10] *Études Carm.*, p. 152.
[11] *Complete Works*, III, p. 45.

that the person who has the stigmata is exempt from all pro-
hibitive psychological blemishes, but that she practises the
Christian virtues of her state, especially humility, obedience,
patience, charity to God and to her neighbour, if not in an
heroic and eminent degree, at least already in excellent manner." [12]

The investigation of these virtues must then be the more
rigorous, as theologians are so doubtful about the possibility of
charismatic stigmatization; for contrary to popular belief, the
stigmata are not a proof of sanctity, but sanctity, or at least
high moral excellence, is the proof of the authenticity of the
stigmata.

In modern times the whole question of stigmatization has
been complicated by the development of the science of psychology. Although formerly theologians were of the opinion
that stigmatization is either of divine (whether mystical or
charismatic) or of diabolic origin, in recent years the view
has been gaining ground that a number of cases are explicable
by purely natural causes. The strange features of stigmatic
wounds, viz. that they refuse to respond to medical treatment,
do not suppurate and are often covered with a thin, protective
film, hold good also for hysterical wounds and hence cannot be
adduced to prove their super- or preternatural origin. Therese
Neumann's bedsores, for example, showed all these signs.[13]
Nor is the fact that such wounds appear in the same places as
the wounds of the Crucified Lord a valid argument against
their natural origin. Professor Waldmann observes on this
point, after recalling several cases of the appearance of wounds
and bleeding in certain determined places of the body caused
by hypnosis, fright neurosis, etc., that "the localization of a
wound in the skin, a bleeding or a blood mark in a definite
place of the body solely by the power of the imagination is
assured." [14] "By the way," he continues a little further on, "if

[12] *Études Carm.*, p. 202f.

[13] Poray-Madeyski, *Le cas de la visionnaire stigmatisée Thérèse Neumann de Konnersreuth*, Paris, 1940, p. 42f.

[14] M. Waldmann in *Theologische Quartalschrift*, Linz/Donau, 1939, p. 564.

one attaches so much importance to the local agreement of the stigmata with the Wounds of Christ, what is to be said of the many cases where this agreement is more or less non-existent, or at least where it has not been there from the beginning? Is not this imperfection, this faultiness of the first stigmatization, and the gradual development of the phenomena a clear proof for the existence of a purely natural psycho-genesis? [15]

But, it is sometimes objected, if certain cases of stigmatization are held to be explicable on purely natural assumptions, how is it that they appear only in the Catholic Church? It seems to us that one explanation would account both for this and also for those spurious visions of the Blessed Virgin, of the Sacred Heart, etc., which occur only within the Catholic Church. Excluding direct diabolic intervention, only the imagination of Catholics is, either consciously or subconsciously, sufficiently saturated with these subjects, and hence predisposed to reproduce them; only in the Western Church has devotion to the Wounds of Christ played a prominent part, hence stigmatization, both genuine and counterfeit, appears in the Catholic Church but not in the Eastern nor in the Protestant sects.[16] In the Eastern Church, on the other hand, there has always been a deep devotion to the Divine Light, hence the phenomenon of Hesychasm, the movement initiated by George Palamas whose adherents claimed to have visions of the Uncreated Light. *Gratia supponit naturam.* God gives at certain times and in certain places particular graces adapted to the circumstances and needs of His creatures; and it is only to be expected that the human imagination—whether consciously or subconsciously—would fix precisely on the forms these graces take in a particular place and time and counterfeit these and not others. Hence it would seem quite fitting that both supernatural stigmatization and its natural counterparts should occur only in the Catholic Church.[17]

[15] *ibid.*, p. 565.

[16] Cf. Prof. Georges Wunderle in *Études Carm.*, Oct., 1936, p. 158.

[17] A case of stigmatization connected with visions of a Protestant Hamburg merchant, said to be " not particularly religious," has recently come to our notice, for which see appendix at the end of this book.

There is a final difficulty: Is not this counterfeiting of supernatural phenomena very disturbing? Is it not disconcerting, even detrimental, to the faith of Catholics thus to throw suspicion on such wonderful occurrences as the reproduction of the Wounds of Our Lord? The answer must be: only if faith is improperly grounded and oriented. As we have indicated in the introduction, it is not only not dangerous to investigate peculiar phenomena, it is most salutary; indeed, this is the very procedure of the Church's most competent authorities in every case of alleged apparitions, private revelations, miracles, etc. But it can be extremely perilous to root one's faith—or perhaps more accurately, one's confidence—in the continual guidance of the Church by the Holy Spirit on unusual phenomena. It is always possible that these may one day be discredited; then those whose faith was closely linked to them will be seriously unsettled. The most prudent course is obviously to preserve the holy indifference and caution in regard to them so constantly recommended by the great Doctors of the Church. It is therefore desirable to attempt to determine with whatever degree of probability circumstances allow whether stigmata (we speak here, of course, of the stigmata of uncanonized persons) are of supernatural or of natural origin.

We have summarized here the signs for a supernatural origin. If, in a stigmatized person, imperfections, especially against humility, fraternal charity, obedience to lawful ecclesiastical authority and so forth are visible; if there appears an unreasonable attachment to visions, revelations and other marks of imagined superiority; if, we say, these are present, then great caution would seem to be demanded before a definite pronouncement is made upon the origin of such stigmatization.

CHAPTER I

Therese Neumann's Early Years

THERESE NEUMANN, the eldest of ten surviving children of a poor country tailor, was born in the Bavarian village of Konnersreuth in 1898. The family were good and pious Catholics of the type so often met with in those parts, who go to Sunday Mass and often to week-day Mass with their Rosary wound round their hard, bony hands, lustily singing hymns throughout the service, unself-consciously kneeling by a way-side crucifix, the *marterl*, and bringing up their children in simplicity and the fear of the Lord. Therese was one of these, and for the first twenty years there is nothing in her life to distinguish her in any way from other Bavarian peasant girls; hence, few facts are recorded of that period.

As a small child she suffered from worms, and while afflicted with this malady showed herself very restless. At the beginning of her third year she was boarded out with an aunt. This aunt describes her as a particularly lively and funny child who could not keep still even for a few seconds to have her photograph taken. When she was six years old she went to the village school, where she showed herself to be an intelligent and attentive pupil who brought home good reports. She received her religious instruction chiefly at the Sunday school, took copious notes of what she had learned, and, like many other children, wept when the story of the Passion was told her. It seems, however, that it did not make much more than the usual surface impression of childhood; for, as Archbishop Teodorowicz tells us, "she looked around in church and was so talkative that her parents punished her by making her kneel on a rough log."[18] In her later years she completed her re-

[18] J. Teodorowicz, *Mystical Phenomena in the Life of Theresa Neumann*, St. Louis, 1947, p. 2. All subsequent references are to this edition.

1

ligious instruction by some private reading, chiefly from the *Imitation*, St. Francis de Sales' *Introduction to the Devout Life*, the review *Notburga* for Catholic servant girls, and the *Rosenhain*, a magazine founded in 1916 by the Salesians of Munich to further the cult of Thérèse of Lisieux, whose *Story of a Soul* she also read.[19]

In 1912, after she had left school, she went into service with a Konnersreuth innkeeper and farmer and worked both in the house and fields, preferring the latter, which gave more scope to her physical energy. In 1917 she was given a real man's job, for she had to look after her employer's oxen. During these years she refused two suitors: once she jumped down from a height of several metres to escape a situation that had become dangerous; on the other occasion she agreed to a meeting but came to it armed with a whip with which she belaboured the would-be lover so thoroughly that he refrained from any further attempts. For she had already chosen her vocation: as soon as the war was over and her help could be spared, she would train to be a missionary sister and go to the negroes.

But her plans were to be upset in an unexpected manner. On the 10th of March, 1918, a Sunday, she had just finished feeding the cattle and was getting ready for the 7:30 Mass, at which she usually received Holy Communion, when a fire broke out in a neighbouring house. According to her own testimony, Therese was seized by such violent fear [20] that she trembled like a child at the sight of the flames. However, she recovered sufficiently to help save the cattle and after that rushed to the threatened house of her employer, who upbraided her for not having come sooner. She went first to her room to save her own clothes and then returned to help extinguish the flames which were already lapping at the roof. Because she was the strongest, she was chosen to stand on a stool and lift pails of water to her employer, who was on the roof and occasionally blamed her for not raising them higher. After two hours of

[19] Poray-Madeyski, p. 4.
[20] Cf. Poray-Madeyski, p. 8.

this work, though yet far from being tired,[21] she suddenly felt a sharp pain in the small of her back. The pail she was just lifting fell from her hands and she had to get down from her stool and leave the scene of the fire.

She then went to the stable to look after the cattle, but was unable to do this; nor could she mount the stairs to her attic. She decided to return home and arrived there bent forward, her body slightly turned to the left, complaining of pains in the small of her back. After a few days' rest she could walk again, though with difficulty; but she could no longer bend forward. Her stomach, too, began to trouble her; she was unable to retain solid food and had to live on liquids and purées; her normal periodical functions were now interrupted. Moreover, a dry, persistent cough, contracted probably because she had kept on her soaked clothing during the fire, gave her considerable pain. It was impossible now for her to carry on her customary duties, yet no one seemed to realize the gravity of her condition; her employer particularly told her rudely that she was just being lazy.

[21] *Ibid.*, p. 9.

CHAPTER II

Illness

S̲O̲ FAR no doctor had been consulted; but soon her state became worse owing to several accidents. For instance, at the beginning of April, 1918, she went into the cellar to bring up some potatoes. When she ascended the stairs with the full basket she fell, hurt the back of her head on a stone step, and lay unconscious for some time. After this fall she had violent pains in her head and complained that her eyes seemed to come out of their sockets. So she once more returned home, and now bowel and bladder troubles began to appear, in consequence of which she soiled her bed, which she had to share with one of her younger sisters. This weakness was an extreme mortification to her. Her mother believed that her young sister was the culprit, and Therese, being very much ashamed, did nothing to clear up the matter.[22]

Quite possibly this event is not important enough to single out for particular mention—a mere childish swerving from truth—yet the majority of Therese Neumann's biographers have insisted again and again on her absolute veracity in all circumstances; so much so that Poray-Madeyski writes of Gerlich: " He tries especially to prove the sincere and constant truthfulness of Therese Neumann in all the circumstances of her life. He makes it a kind of axiom: what Therese Neumann says replaces all other proof. All the ' Circle of Konnersreuth ' accept implicitly this thesis." [23]

As her continued bad health caused her naturally gay temper to become somewhat morose, Therese's mother decided to

[22] F. Gerlich, *Die stigmatisierte Therese von Konnersreuth.* 2 vols. Muenchen, 1929. I, p. 35.
[23] Poray-Madeyski, p. 146.

4

remove her to the hospital at Waldsassen, the nearest town, which she entered on April 23rd. There she conceived at once a strong dislike for the doctor who examined her, and spoke to him only of her backache and of a feeling that a tight cord was wound round her waist, but did not mention her other ailments. On her own testimony, she contrived to hide her internal troubles even from the nurses attending her. She also disobeyed the doctor's orders to keep to a strict diet of liquids by eating the bread and butter and other things her family brought her. After seven weeks, when she could no longer endure the enforced inactivity of the hospital (recall the early restlessness) where she felt as if she were shut up in a cage,[24] she returned home against the advice of the hospital authorities.

Already in the hospital Therese had been suffering from convulsive spasms which were usually brought about by some slight touch or tension on a particularly sensitive spot in the lumbar region, and these fits continued to occur frequently. About the same time she received another serious shock, this time rather mental than physical: her old doctor remarked that she might have a sudden and complete breakdown. These words seemed to shatter all her hopes of a missionary vocation. From now on her state of health deteriorated still further; the convulsive spasms became an almost daily occurrence and lasted sometimes for hours. Once she even remained for six days in a state of lethargy [25] with her breathing reduced to almost complete imperceptibility. After yet another fall, her sight became worse, large regions of her skin lost all sensitivity, and her parents decided to consult another doctor. When he prescribed an absolute rest for three months, this period seemed too long to Therese's father and consequently Dr. Seidl, a friend of the parish priest, Fr. Naber, undertook to treat her. He too ordered rest and gave her sedatives, but her convulsions continued with undiminished force and frequency, often throwing her out of bed and usually developing into a state of semi-consciousness.

[24] *ibid.*, p. 14.
[25] Gerlich, I, p. 35.

One day her mother noticed two small protuberances in the region of her spine, which were observed also by a nursing sister. The latter told Fr. Naber about them, who afterwards said to Therese that unless this place of her spine was healed, all medical treatment would be in vain.[26] Thus arose the story that Therese was suffering from a dislocation of two lumbar vertebrae, a fact not noted by any of the doctors who had examined her,[27] but stated by most of her biographers.[28]

Meanwhile her accidents continued, due to the lack of sufficient rest in a busy household. Moreover, "she could never resign herself to remaining quietly in bed, nor would she refrain from participating in the childish games of her little brothers."[29] After one such seizure, in March, 1919, she lost her eyesight, and the conjunctiva and cornea became completely insensitive so that they could be touched without even a flutter of the eyelids. Yet the pupils reacted quite normally to the light.[30] This, according to Poray-Madeyski, in combination with the absence of sensitivity just mentioned, indicates that there was nothing organically wrong with her eyes, that the blindness was of hysterical origin. H. J. Urban, professor of neuropsychiatry at Innsbruck, in an article reproduced in *The Catholic Review* for March, 1948, rejects this interpretation. His article is, however, cursory and sometimes inaccurate and cannot be compared with the thorough investigation made by the medical expert of the Sacred Congregation of Rites, Dr. Poray-Madeyski. Urban writes in one place of "her complete abstinence from food of any kind since she was eighteen (1927)[31] whereas, since Therese was born in 1898, she would have been at that time 29.

During the years of blindness that followed, Therese relied more than ever on the games of the children to while away the time. This seemed to contribute considerably to the frequency

[26] Poray-Madeyski, p. 27.

[27] *ibid.*, p. 27.

[28] F. Von Lama, *Therese Neumann,* Amer. trans. 1936, p. 15; Gerlich II, p. 393, reproduced by Teodorowicz, p. 114.

[29] Poray-Madeyski, p. 28.

[30] *ibid.*, p. 29 and 210ff.

[31] *ibid.*, p. 31.

of her accidents. It is significant, and would again suggest
hysteria, that changes in the sensibility and motility of her
limbs, as well as changes in the course of her illness generally,
always took place after one of her convulsive fits.[32] Thus, after
leaning out of bed in order to get some grains for her pigeon,
her whole left side became paralysed; she could neither hear
with her left ear nor speak, and was in such a state of nervous
excitement that she could not bear to be touched by anyone
except her mother.

Her dumbness as well as her partial deafness began gradually to disappear, probably, suggests Poray-Madeyski, under
the influence of her mother's tears; [33] but the lameness and
blindness remained. A remarkable incident took place in the
summer of 1919. Her father, during his war service, had
gained some experience in medical matters and was of the
opinion that she could move if she wanted to, since there was
nothing organically wrong with her. Thus, one day he told
her to try to sit in a chair. Helped by her mother, he lifted
Therese out of bed and held her on either side, with the effect
that she fell unconscious into her parents' arms and became so
rigid that she could not be moved. After this experience her
father gave up all further attempts.[34] As a consequence of the
accident, both her legs became paralysed as well.

Since Therese had now for some time been unable to work,
she applied for a pension. In February, 1920, four doctors,
among them Dr. Seidl, signed the report required for this. In
it they unanimously deny any external injury and give as the
cause of her being an invalid "*very grave hysteria with blindness and partial paralysis*," which had appeared in consequence
of the shock sustained at the fire.[35]

This report is worthy of the closest consideration. First of
all, it was given in 1920, that is to say, three years before the
beginning of the cures and six years before the stigmatization.
Thus, the doctors had no motive whatever to conceal any pos-

[32] *ibid.*, p. 31.
[33] *ibid.*, p. 33.
[34] *ibid.*, p. 35.
[35] *ibid.*, p. 36.

sible supernatural phenomena by the term hysteria. On the contrary, the doctors who wrote the report had every reason to diagnose an organic disease, since the Insurance would be much more likely to grant their patient a pension in the case of an organic, rather than of a nervous, disease. If the four doctors who treated Therese were unanimous in diagnosing "very grave hysteria" in such a case, they must have been unable to find an organic cause, and in any serious discussion of Therese Neumann their judgment ought to be accorded its proper importance as evidence.

Before, then, approaching the period in which extraordinary phenomena begin to appear, the results of our preliminary investigation are: on the physical plane, a series of illnesses attributed to grave hysteria by the doctors consulted; on the moral plane, no visible outstanding virtues, but several imperfections combined with the sincere piety of an ordinary Catholic peasant girl.

CHAPTER III

Miraculous Cures

FROM CHRISTMAS, 1922, Therese had suffered from particularly painful gastric troubles that prevented her from taking anything but liquid food and frequently caused vomitings of blood. On the 25th of April, 1923, she had an unusually violent vomiting attack; these conditions continued during the following days. On Sunday, April 29th, therefore, her father decided to give up his Sunday rest and to travel to Neustadt, where he would consult a herbalist who had already helped his daughter from time to time. At six o'clock in the morning, before departing, he went to say goodbye to Therese. Half an hour later she opened her eyes and could see. She attributed this cure to Thérèse of the Child Jesus, in honour of whose coming beatification she had just begun a novena. When the family doctor was told about the cure and its interpretation next day, his only comment was: " Yes, that may be so."

The story of the astonishing event spread rapidly in the neighbourhood; but when the Carmelite Fathers at Regensburg asked Father Naber whether it could be counted as a miracle in the future canonization process of the new Beata, he replied in the negative; in fact, Therese had not asked for the cure.[36]

Poray-Madeyski, after establishing in a meticulous and painstaking analysis that the blindness, as the examining doctors had affirmed in their report, was indeed caused by hysteria, concludes that " the sudden return of visual perception . . . which explains itself in a perfectly natural manner, *can on no*

[36] Poray-Madeyski, p. 40f.

account be considered a miraculous fact." [37]   For "one of the
particular features proper to hysteria . . . is the faculty, common to all the manifestations of this neurosis, to disappear as
suddenly as they have appeared, whatever their apparent
gravity and duration." [38]   It is this strange characteristic of the
disease that leads the layman so frequently to believe in a
miraculous intervention where there has been none; and the
extreme prudence of the Church in these matters, which so
forcibly strikes the reader of Benedict XIV's great work *De
Beatificatione* or of any process of beatification, is a very necessary safeguard, especially in modern times when unbelievers
choose to sneer at the credulity of Catholics who attribute to
supernatural intervention phenomena known to any medical
expert.

We would repeat in this context the words of Professor J.
L'hermitte in his introduction to Poray-Madeyski's book:
"Contrary to certain spirits who maintain even today that it is
lacking in respect to the Deity . . . to apply merciless criticism to miraculous phenomena, we must follow the direction
of the head of the Church (sc. Benedict XIV), who not only
authorizes, but advises us to observe meticulously all the facts
that might seem abnormal and disconcerting, and to seek per-
severingly a natural origin and explanation." [39]   We believe,
then, that we may safely follow Poray-Madeyski, the expert of
the Congregation of Rites, in rejecting the miraculous nature
of Therese Neumann's first cure.

Though her blindness had disappeared, the other complaints
still remained. In summer, 1924, she had several abscesses in
her throat, ears, etc., which opened and discharged matter
spontaneously. Her convulsions, too, continued, and it appears
from all the accounts that she took no precautions to avoid
them. But owing to her natural impetuosity, there occurred
one fit after another, especially when she leaned out of bed to
play with her little brothers. Her biographer, Gerlich, remarks on this carelessness which Poray-Madeyski, basing himself on the investigations of Pierre Janet, considers one of the

[37] *ibid.*, p. 245; his italics.
[38] *ibid.*, p. 244.
[39] *ibid.*, p. xii.

characteristics of hysteria, usually manifested in an indifference to the state of health and, indeed, to everything that does not fall within the scope of the hysteric's particular preoccupations.[40]

One especially violent fit at the close of the summer of 1924 resulted in a grave muscular contraction. Her left leg was so drawn up under her right thigh that it could not be moved from this position. Since she was now obliged to lie constantly on her back, she developed bedsores. The family doctor failed to cure them, though they frequently healed quite naturally in the course of time. One rather serious wound developed on the left foot; it lingered so persistently that Therese's mother began to fear that it might have to be amputated. Her continued alarm aroused Therese, who decided at length to pray for a cure.

This is how Witt describes the "miracle" worked on this wound, using the account of Therese Neumann herself: "My sister, Zenzl, had once more put a fresh dressing on the foot. In the evening of the *next day* we placed the rose leaves [41] beneath the bandages. At first I did not notice any change. But after a few minutes I felt a strong irritation on the bad spot, and the pain had gone. I asked my sister to open the bandages. But she had no time and did not think it necessary to change the dressing again. Therefore, I had to be patient till next morning. When we removed the dressing we found it stuck to the bedclothes on account of blood and matter . . . As my sister now removes the bandage, she looks at the foot: a new, though still thin, skin had formed which looked bluish. The three rose leaves were glued to the bandage by the blood and matter." [42]

It is this cure which Archbishop Teodorowicz, whilst admitting the possibility of a natural explanation for the others, retains as undoubtedly miraculous. "Among the cures of Theresa Neumann's ailments," he writes, "one possesses a

[40] Poray-Madeyski, p. 202f.

[41] These petals had touched the tomb of St. Thérèse of Lisieux.

[42] Witt, p. 83; my italics. Cf. Archbishop Teodorowicz's account, p. 125 his book, where the quotation from Witt has been changed regarding the time lapse between application of dressing and its removal.

supernatural character that stands without doubt: the cure of deep sores. Their sudden and complete cure can in no way be explained by natural means. Three things are certain about Theresa's sores: (1) there were deep sores on her left foot and on her back. I have made inquiries about them, but Theresa's own remarks . . . about these sores are sufficient to make the matter clear to us; (2) the most varied remedies proved ineffective and at best brought the patient only temporary relief; (3) these sores suddenly healed and left no scars." [43]

Yet this cure, too, is rejected by the medical authority of the Congregation of Rites: " The wound localized in the region of the ankle," writes Poray-Madeyski, " was not deep, nor could it be so. After the description of Witt and Gerlich, what was affected here was, at the most, the deeper layers of the epidermis and not the dermis itself. This is demonstrated by the kind of secretion, serous and sanguinolent as well as purulent . . . which indicates the angioneurotic origin of the lesion, which accounts for its tenacity and its resistance to all treatment; but it is precisely this origin which disposed it to heal spontaneously and quickly. The healing, that is to say the fact that the wound covered itself again with a fine bluish pellicular film, was seen only about thirty-six hours after the last dressing, which is an interval quite sufficient to produce such an epithelial pellicle *in a perfectly natural way.* This cure . . . then, *cannot be regarded as miraculous.*" [44] The very fact that the wounds left no scars, considered by Teodorowicz as evidence of their miraculous cure, is given by Poray-Madeyski as a further demonstration of its natural character: " During more than five years," he writes, " a number of these wounds (i.e. the bedsores) healed one by one spontaneously, in a perfectly natural and naturally explicable manner, and like the wound of the ankle, they covered themselves again with a tiny epithelial pellicle, *without leaving proper scars.*" [45]

[43] Teodorowicz, p. 124.
[44] Poray-Madeyski, p. 246f.; his italics.
[45] *ibid.*, p. 248.

CHAPTER IV

Visions and Voices

S O FAR the cures of Therese had occurred suddenly, without accompanying extraordinary manifestations. But on May 17th, 1925, the day of the Canonization of Thérèse of Lisieux, a new phenomenon made its appearance. In the afternoon of this day, Therese's parents heard her cry out loud and came running into her room. There they saw her looking fixedly at the wall, her eyes wide open and her expression radiant with joy; apparently talking with some invisible being. Suddenly she, who had been lying in bed paralysed for years, was sitting up extending her hands, and afterwards fell back on her bed. When her mother tidied her bedclothes she noticed to her amazement that Therese's left leg had recovered its normal position and was lying stretched out beside the other.

Meanwhile, the parish priest had arrived and asked her where she had been. By way of answer she told him she was now able to walk. She had a dress brought her and actually left her bed and made a few steps in her room, assisted by her father and a nursing Sister. After getting back into bed she told Fr. Naber that, while reciting the Rosary, at the mystery of the Ascension, she had suddenly seen a brilliant light, out of which came a voice asking: "Resl, would you like to get well?" She answered that all was the same to her, to get well, to remain ill, or to die, according to God's will.[46] But the voice continued: "Resl, would you not be glad if you could at least sit up and walk?" To which she gave a similar answer as before. Then the voice came a third time, telling her that she

---

[46] Note the apparent perfect resignation, which may be due either to an advanced state of perfection or . . . to the habitual indifference of the hysteric to her state of health.

was allowed to have a little joy today, she could sit up. And she felt herself taken by the hand and raised, feeling at the same time a sharp pain in the sensitive spot of her spine. Then the voice continued: "You will have still much more to suffer, and no doctor will be able to help you. But fear nothing. I have helped you so far, and I will help you further. It is only through suffering that you can realize your vocation of victim, and assist priests. Many more souls have been saved through suffering than by the finest sermons. I have written this before." And the voice added: "Now you can walk." After these words the light disappeared; and Therese found herself in bed, surrounded by her parents, Fr. Naber, and a nursing Sister. During the time the vision had lasted she had been looking in the direction of a picture of St. Thérèse. When the Sister afterwards examined her back she found that her spine was once more perfectly normal, and that all the sores were healed.[47] From this time Therese could walk, though only leaning on a stick and with a limp, for the left leg seemed slightly shorter than the right one. This means that the "cure" was far from complete. She also was unable to do any work except knitting, and her digestion became so bad that she could hardly retain even liquid food.

At this stage, then, appears for the first time a vision in connection with a "cure," and the question of its origin must be discussed. Is it natural or supernatural? Two weighty reasons can be adduced for the latter view. Therese Neumann, on the unanimous testimony of all who knew her, is not an imaginative type of person; hence it is unlikely that the vision should have been a figment of her imagination. Secondly, the voice in the vision announced the cure, and the cure actually did take place. Hence it is concluded that both vision and cure were of a supernatural character.

There is, however, another point of view. It is an established fact that, at the time of this first vision, Therese Neumann was still subject to spasms and convulsions which after-

---

[47] Our account of the cure follows Poray-Madeyski, pp. 44-50, which is based on those of Gerlich and Witt; the work of the latter author has not been consulted by me.

wards disappeared. Thus, the medical expert is perfectly
within his rights if he tries to find a natural explanation for
both vision and change, within the context of the disease.
This is the interpretation offered by Poray-Madeyski: "The
most adequate explanation of the luminous visions of Therese,
and one that appears to be perfectly evident, is that for the
spasmodic crisis there was now substituted the immixture of
phenomena of a *cataleptic state* as an *equivalent,* in the course
of which this state revealed itself as dominant by the sudden
apparition of its ordinary attribute, i.e. a visual and auditive
hallucination." [48] Here we have, then, the surprising explanation of a physician, in no wise prejudiced against the supernatural, who considers the whole complex of vision, audition
and cure as an expression of the development of Therese's
nervous disease towards the state of catalepsy, defined by the
Oxford Dictionary as a "disease in which trances occur."

But, even though the medical expert diagnoses catalepsy,
may not the theologian consider a supernatural explanation
more adequate? This is the opinion of Archbishop Teodorowicz, who writes: "The words spoken to Theresa were under-
standable, and that even to the smallest detail, as for example:
'Through your (the 'your' seems to be an addition of the
author; it is left out in the accounts of other writers and in
Teodorowicz's own on p. 147) suffering far more souls will be
saved than through the most brilliant sermons.' But Theresa,"
continues Teodorowicz, "knew nothing of the person or of a
letter which this person is supposed to have written, and much
less of the excerpt from one of these letters. Not only did she
know nothing about this excerpt, but she could not have read
it anywhere, because no book containing the exact biography
of the little saint could be found in her home or in the rectory.
Theresa, who, in her report of this excerpt, did not know to
whom it referred, said about it: 'The voice did not mention
any name to me.' Yet Theresa and the persons around her
were most eager to know who was the person that wrote these
words in the letter. Search was made in the family circle, and

[48] Poray-Madeyski, p. 250f.; italics his.

the pastor was also taken into their confidence. ' But,' Theresa reports, ' none of us knew who wrote the sentence. The next day the pastor found it in the writings of St. Thérèse of the Child Jesus, which he himself did not possess but borrowed.' Theresa's train of thought," concludes Teodorowicz, " is unexplainable unless we suppose a higher intervention." [49]

The Archbishop's argumentation, however, is not without its weaknesses. The statement that " she could not have read it anywhere, because no book containing the exact biography of the little saint could be found in her home or in the rectory " may be questioned. We know that Therese read regularly the magazine " Rosenhain " and other literature on the Saint,[50] and there seems to be no reason why she should not have read this phrase somewhere else than in an " exact biography," even though no book containing it was at that particular time to be found in her home or in the Presbytery. It is quite possible that in her waking state she should have forgotten both the words and their source; it is a common experience that people often remember things in dreams of which they would never have thought again in full consciousness.

It is, moreover, significant that Therese should have remembered precisely these words. As we shall find repeatedly in the course of her later life, she does not like scholarship. On the other hand, she had the desire to save souls; but her original intention of becoming a Missionary Sister it was now impossible to realize. What is more natural than that the words of St. Thérèse should have sunk into her subconscious memory, because they seemed to provide a way of realizing her desire after all, though in a different way from the one she had anticipated? We therefore find it necessary to accept with caution the statement of the Archbishop that " Theresa's train of thought is inexplicable unless we suppose a higher intervention." On the contrary, an alternative solution is equally acceptable: the quotation revealed that sermons could be subordinated to suffering as a means of saving souls; suffering, which she has, then appears superior to scholarship, which

[49] Teodorowicz, p. 148f.
[50] Gerlich, I, p. 1ff.

she has not. Even though she might have forgotten the passage after reading it, it could quite possibly have been treasured up in a deeper layer of her memory to spring up again at the appropriate time. Admittedly, this is a supposition and not conclusive; however, it would seem to indicate that the medical explanation of the vision should not be too readily rejected.

A further cure took place on September 30th, the anniversary of the death of St. Thérèse. About midnight, Therese Neumann saw the same light as before and heard the same voice telling her that she could now walk without any help, but that she would have to suffer more. The voice added that she should obey her confessor blindly and preserve childlike simplicity.

The suffering announced in the vision came in November. During the night of the 6th to the 7th she had a temptation against her readiness to submit to more suffering. This threw her into a state of intense agitation, resulting in abundant perspiration.[51] As she feared to be late for Mass in the morning, she did not change her linen which had become quite damp. Later on in the day she felt so ill that she retired to bed thinking she had caught a cold. For the next three days she was in a state of complete nervous prostration, unable even to open her eyes.[52] In the evening of November 13th, Dr. Seidl came and diagnosed acute appendicitis, which necessitated an immediate operation. We give the sequel in the words of Fr. Naber:

"After consulting with Dr. Seidl, I told the parents they ought to consider the physician's verdict as the voice of God and have their daughter taken to hospital at once . . . The invalid called me to her bedside and asked whether she might not beg little Saint Thérèse to help her, so that she would not have to be operated on, if such were the will of God. Not, she declared, that she objected to the operation, but because her mother was lamenting so inconsolably. When I answered

---

[51] Poray-Madeyski, p. 51. Gerlich I, p. 95.
[52] Cf. Fr. Naber's account cited by Von Lama, *op. cit.*, p. 37.

Yes, she had a relic of St. Thérèse placed on the painful spot, and while those present prayed to the Little Flower, the invalid in her bed turned like a worm in agony . . . All of a sudden, Therese sat up and opened her eyes. Her face became as transfigured. She lifted up her hands and stretched them out toward an invisible object, and was heard to say a few times, ' Yes.' Then she sat up completely and pressed her fingers against the abdomen repeatedly, and said, ' Really.' I asked her whether Saint Thérèse had, perhaps, come again and helped her. The answer was, ' Yes, and she told me I must go to church at once and thank God. Mother, bring me a dress.' All pain and all fever had disappeared. The same Light and the same Voice had come again, and the Voice had said: ' Your complete submission and joyous endurance of pain pleases us. That the world may know that there is a Higher Power, you shall not have to be operated on. Arise and go to church, but at once, at once, and thank the Lord . . .' " [53]   Von Lama continues: " And so a little procession of ten persons . . . wended its way, with Therese in the centre, across the village square and entered the church. Meanwhile, the news had spread and the villagers flocked to the Neumann house. Each one wished to hear tell of this miracle. It was late before quiet could be restored." [54]

We have quoted this story at length because it is very illuminating, both from the medical and from the psychological point of view. As Poray-Madeyski points out,[55] after the cure in September all Therese's complaints, blindness, paralysis, anæsthesia, convulsions, etc., had disappeared, and her biographers say nothing more about them. She ought, therefore, to have recovered her former health and capacity for work. This, however, was not the case. Gerlich tells us that the only work she could do was knitting.[56] Now if, as he sets out to prove, her illness had been due to purely physical causes, why, when the illnesses had disappeared, was there still this general

[53] *ibid.*, p. 37.
[54] *ibid.*, p. 39.
[55] p. 257.
[56] Gerlich I, p. 49.

weakness that incapacitated her for a normal life? "One sole
disease," writes Poray-Madeyski, "can be the reason: the
disease that was first diagnosed by Dr. Seidl and three other
expert doctors and later confirmed by eminent medical authorities, viz. hysteria. Hysteria in its grave and classical form.
This diagnosis is the only one that, as says Dr. Masoin, 'dominates all, because it accounts for all'; it explains the cures of
1923 and 1925 as well as the state of Therese Neumann following these cures, and *all*[57] that took place afterwards.
This is so because, as is stressed by Professor Van Gehuchten,
from the disappearance of one hysterical manifestation one
cannot conclude to the disappearance or cure of the hysteria
itself; this latter persists, and its presence will reveal itself,
sooner or later, in another form on the occasion of the slightest
emotion."[58]

Now according to this expert medical opinion the general
weakness, one of the principal permanent characteristics of
hysteria, remained with Therese, and soon the disease manifested itself once more in the way just recounted. The emotion
that led to a renewed outbreak can be explained by the
temptation against submission to more suffering—indeed, it
was so strong that it caused her whole body to be covered with
perspiration and resulted in a state of complete collapse in
which she could not so much as open her eyes. At the same
time she began to feel intense abdominal pains. Poray-
Madeyski, after a detailed technical examination of the symptoms that led Dr. Seidl—the only doctor to examine her—to
diagnose acute appendicitis, comes to the following conclusion:
"All these symptoms are hardly sufficient to admit the presence of acute appendicitis in an ordinary case, i.e. in a patient
of a normal nervous system; but they must be considered
altogether insufficient to determine its existence where a
neuropathic hysterical subject is concerned. Hysteria, the great
mimic of all organic affections, can also give an imitation of
almost all splanchnic affections, including acute appendicitis

[57] His italics.
[58] Poray-Madeyski, p. 257.

and peritonitis. Hence the great difficulty of a correct diagnosis in hysterical cases and the great frequency of errors.[59] But," he continues, " what gives to the clinical picture a specific feature is the fact, expressly noted in the account of Fr. Naber and repeated by Gerlich and Witt, that during all the discussions between Dr. Seidl and her parents . . . ' she writhed with pain like a worm in her bed '; she would certainly not have been in a state to do this if there had been a case of real acute purulent appendicitis." [60]

Anyone who has ever suffered from this or a similar complaint will endorse the physician's statement that, in such a case, the patient takes care to avoid even the slightest movements on account of the excruciating pains they would cause. " This fact alone," says Poray-Madeyski, " *suffices perfectly to exclude in the most categorical manner* the diagnosis, already uncertain in itself, which Dr. Seidl hastily formulated in the home of the Neumanns, where conditions are so little favourable to observation, on a deficient symptomatology and with an incontestably hysterical subject." [61]

This, then, helps to account for the disease—but what of the cure? Poray-Madeyski gives his conclusion: " Following in its turn a lively two-fold emotion, caused as much by the lamentations of her mother as by the fear of an imminent operation, the *sudden disappearance* of all morbid phenomena, in complete harmony with the essential character of the neurosis, was then its *natural consequence*. This lively notion, however, provokes at the same time the appearance of a very characteristic accessory crisis, which is so often added . . . at the end of various hysterical crises . . . by the admixture of cataleptic states, with their typical visual and auditory hallucinations . . . Such a cataleptic state, an equivalent of the one of September 30th, revealed itself by an analogous visual and auditory hallucination and a similar characteristic attitude of Therese: with open eyes, hands stretched out towards the object which she seemed to see, attentive and happy play of

[59] *ibid.*, p. 258f.; his italics.
[60] *ibid.*, p. 265.
[61] *ibid.*, p. 265; his italics.

the features . . ." [62] Hence he concludes: "This episode, so characteristic, of the pretended cure of what was so clearly pseudo-appendicitis, as it results from the objective analysis, ought not to be regarded as a miraculous event, even by a very naive (*ingénu*) or very indulgent observer. This sole episode, by the way, would in itself be completely sufficient to establish with all security the diagnosis of hysteria for Therese Neumann, even in the absence of all other specific signs of the neurosis." [63]

After the argumentation of the physician we would once more cite Archbishop Teodorowicz, who first quotes Von Lama's account: "Voice: 'Your entire self-renunciation and willingness to suffer pleases us. That the world may know that there is a higher intervention, you will not have to be operated on now. You should get up and go to church, but at once and immediately thank the Lord. You will have to suffer much, but you need not fear, not even the interior suffering. Only thus can you cooperate in the salvation of souls. But you must always die to yourself. Always remain childlike and simple.' These visions," continues Teodorowicz, "cannot be traced to autosuggestion, which is always the echo of one's own wishes and imaginations; it is especially impossible to trace the form of Theresa's vision." [64]

But is autosuggestion the only alternative? Accepting for the moment Poray-Madeyski's hypothesis that this vision has its origin in Therese's hysteria, it does, indeed, seem susceptible of a quite different interpretation. There is first the compliment to herself: "Your entire self-renunciation and willingness to suffer pleases us." The "Voice" leaves little room for improvement; her self-denial and readiness to suffer are already perfect. Then the "Voice" continues: "That the world may know that there is a higher intervention, you will not have to be operated on now." Here one may ask: could "the world" which failed to acknowledge a higher interven-

[62] *ibid.*, p. 266; his italics.
[63] *ibid.*, p. 267.
[64] Teodorowicz, p. 147f.

tion at Lourdes or Fatima be compelled to do so now by a cure which the expert of the Holy See emphatically rejects? It has been suggested that it is in perfect harmony with the psychology of hysteria (as well as of simple religious day-dreaming) that the subject should see herself as the centre and cause of a world-wide religious revival. But as this dream cannot be realized at the moment, she must content herself with being at the centre of a very much smaller movement.

There is in this incident an incongruous element, the im-probability of which reinforces the medical arguments of Poray-Madeyski. For the darkness, the hiddenness, the pain-ful contradictions in which the Saints start their supernatural course, there are here substituted limelight and publicity: Therese moves into the centre of the stage to the accompani-ment of praise from her mysterious " Voice " and approval from her director.

CHAPTER V

Stigmatization

D URING THE months following the events related in the last chapter there were no more extraordinary happenings. Early in 1926, Therese had several minor complaints, among them an abscess in her right ear. About this time, too, there began to ooze from her eyes a blood-coloured serum mingled with pus.[65] All during Lent, 1926, she had to stay in bed on account of her exceptional feebleness which increased during Holy Week, when she was incapable even of thinking about the Passion or remembering which day of the week it was. In this state of complete physical and spiritual prostration she had the first of her visions of the Passion. This is how her biographer, F. Von Lama, describes it: " It was during the Lent of 1926, at night, and Therese lay quietly in her bed without giving a thought to anything in particular. She could not because of her suffering. 'All at once,' she says, 'I saw the Redeemer before me. I saw Him in the Garden of Mount Olive. When this happened to me the first time, I did not know that it had a special meaning. But I saw the Saviour as He knelt there . . . Suddenly I felt, while I saw the Saviour, such a pain in my side that I thought, now I am going to die. At the same time I felt something hot run down my side. It was blood. It kept trickling until towards noon of the next day. From Friday noon onward, the whole next week was quiet.'[66] After the vision had ceased, her state of languor continued unchanged.

" Next week, during the night from Thursday to Friday,

[65] This phenomenon is not unknown in women whose normal periodical functions have been interrupted.

[66] Von Lama, p. 47f.

Therese had again the vision of Our Lord in the Garden, and in addition one of the scourging. The wound in the side began to bleed again. In the visions of the following Fridays she saw Our Lord crowned with thorns and the carrying of the Cross to Calvary. During this last vision there appeared on the *back* of her left hand, *in a place where some days before she had noticed a red spot,* an open wound which began to bleed. During the visions of Maundy Thursday blood, still mingled with pus, flowed from Therese's eyes, and her state seemed so critical that Fr. Naber came to administer the Last Sacraments. When asked whether she was going to die, she replied in the affirmative. On regaining consciousness she felt intense pains in her hands and feet, on the backs of which open wounds had appeared. 'I do not know exactly when I got them,' she avowed. 'On Good Friday night they were simply there . . . During the vision I did not have the least intimation of them, for I was not thinking at all of myself. How could I? I could do nothing but look at the Saviour. When I . . . came to again, I felt that blood was running down my hands and feet, too. I could not see what it was, however, because of the blood which closed my eyes. Not until at night did I say to my sister, "Zenzl, see what is the matter with my hands and feet, they hurt me so much.'" Therese's parents called Fr. Naber. He said to her: 'In obedience let me see the wounds of your hands and feet.' What he saw moved him so vehemently that it required considerable time for him to regain his composure." [67]

This account of Therese's stigmatization, given by one of her earliest admirers, presents certain contrasts to the stigmatization of the canonized Saints of the Church, a St. Francis, a St. Catherine of Siena, a St. Gemma Galgani, to name but three of the best known. All these were in their ordinary state of health when receiving the Sacred Wounds, and all were at prayer while it happened. St. Francis was praying on Mount Alvernia, St. Catherine was making her thanksgiving after Mass in the church of Santa Cristina at Pisa, St. Gemma

[67] *ibid.*, p. 49; my italics.

Galgani was making the Holy Hour at home. Therese Neumann, we are told, was lying in bed in a state of such complete prostration that she did not know the day of the week,[68] "without giving thought to anything in particular."[69] The three Saints mentioned above knew what was taking place, and the exact moment when it occurred; moreover, they received the stigmata in almost exactly the same manner: while rapt in ecstasy, Our Lord—or in the case of St. Francis, the "crucified Seraph"—appeared to them with His Wounds open, from which issued rays which touched their hands, feet and heart, causing them intense pain. Therese, however, tells us: "I do not know exactly when I got them. On Good Friday night they were simply there." And she adds: "During the vision I did not have the least intimation of them for I was not thinking at all of myself."

There is another significant note: Therese's wounds were not impressed all at once, as in the case of the Saints, but developed gradually. Teodorowicz speaks of the "gradual appearance of the stigmata in Theresa Neumann."[70] First, in the night from the 4th to the 5th of March, 1926, blood oozed from her left side near her heart. Then, during the Friday vision of March 26th, there appeared an open wound on the back of her left hand, and only during the Good Friday visions of April 2nd were there also wounds on the outside of the right hand and on both feet. The wounds on the insides of hands and feet, as well as the marks of the Crown of Thorns and the shoulder wound, appeared much later.

Of these two great differences the first seems to us the more important. All the graces given for the sanctification of one's own soul or of the souls of others are intimately connected with the operations of the Holy Ghost. Now of the gifts of the Holy Ghost, those of wisdom and understanding are the most essential for the spiritual life, and when great graces are bestowed on a soul, an intellectual illumination is generally given with them. This does not mean that the soul must realize at

[68] Witt I, p. 179, cited by Poray-Madeyski.
[69] Von Lama, p. 47.
[70] p. 283.

once the full importance and consequences of the grace, but she will always be sufficiently aware of what is happening to perceive its meaning, at least in a general way. This is particularly true if the grace is of a very elevated order. While it is not impossible that a human being should be conformed to the Incarnate Word of God while in a state of mental prostration, it is a deviation from the usual and familiar operations of the Holy Spirit. "Such a state of apathy and intellectual torpor," writes Poray-Madeyski, "from which it is difficult to free the patient . . . is precisely one of the classical prodromic phenomena of hysterical paroxysms . . . With such a paroxysm there can be associated, with its typical hallucinations, a *cataleptic state which then dominates the morbid scene.* It is exactly thus, in such conditions, in correspondence with such a prodromic state, *the psychic equivalent of a specific paroxysm,* that the first of her 'historical' visions appeared in Therese Neumann." [71]

Poray-Madeyski, then, sees in the whole complex of extraordinary phenomena that appeared during Lent and Passion Tide, 1926, no more than a renewed outbreak of the old disease in a somewhat different form; and this interpretation would seem to explain the absence of any supernatural illumination that we have already noted. A similar view is held by Professor M. Waldmann (Regensburg) who writes in an article on the *Problem of Stigmatization* as follows: ". . . . there is another possibility to distinguish cases of charismatic Stigmatization from those of a hypnotic-hysterical kind. One often reads in accounts of 'stigmatized persons' that these had no idea of their bleedings and marks until their attention was drawn to them by others. The believing devotees emphasize this fact approvingly as an argument against an artificial production of the Stigmatization. But they do not know how much precisely this circumstance proves a purely natural, psychogenic origin of such bloodmarks, and contradicts the supernatural, charismatic character." [72]

---

[71] Poray-Madeyski, p. 270; his italics.
[72] M. Waldmann, "Zum Problem der Stigmatization," in *Theologisch-praktische Quartalschrift,* Linz, 1939, p. 571f.

Perhaps at this point it may be useful to examine further the circumstances of the stigmatization of the saints previously mentioned. St. Francis received the Stigmata two years before his death, when he had arrived at the summit of sanctity and was inebriated with love of the Crucified; his soul, as St. Francis de Sales says, "having been all transformed into a second Crucifix." [73] St. Catherine, too, was at the height of her mystic and apostolic life: stigmatization was but the seal set upon a soul that lived wholly for Christ and Him crucified. And for Gemma Galgani there is her own description of how Our Lord prepared her for the grace a few days before she actually received it. "I found myself," she writes, "in the presence of Jesus Crucified, blood flowing from His Wounds. The sight filled me with pain. I lowered my eyes and made the sign of the Cross: I felt great peace of mind, but still intense sorrow for my sins. I had not the courage to look at Jesus. I bent down with forehead to the ground and remained so for several hours . . . when I came to myself the wounds of Jesus were so impressed on my mind that they have never since left it."

In the case of these saints, then, the condition of St. John of the Cross is fulfilled. The stigmata are but the external signs of the interior wound of love. What proof do we have that this condition is also fulfilled in the case of Therese Neumann?

The most reliable and complete source of information on her spiritual life is the book of Archbishop Teodorowicz, which we will therefore cite on this point. He informs us that: "the mystical life and the mystical graces of Theresa Neumann begin only after her stigmatization." And he goes on: "Theresa herself says that she did not feel any of the mystical experiences within her before her stigmatization, that only afterward did they become fully a part of her. The pastor (i.e. Father Naber), too, as he told me, never thought that this very sick person could be in a mystical state. He saw in her only an example of a good Christian submitting to the will of God; not an exception, but rather one of the many that practise the

---

[73] *Traité de l'Amour de Dieu*, Bk. 6, Ch. 15.

virtue of Christian patience and submit to the will of God—
nothing beyond that. What in her pointed to the future was
made up of that practical foundation of which all Christian
lives are composed. There was no indication of mysticism or
of any particular devotion. It would be useless to seek for
some connection between her known, circumscribed past and
her later mystical life." [74]

These statements are admirably clear and direct, as well as
illuminating this particular difficulty. Whatever may be the
exact connotation of the word mysticism in this context—it
seems that both Fr. Naber and Mgr. Teodorowicz mean by it
the external phenomena of visions and ecstasies—it appears
from these words that the spiritual life of Therese was that of
the average practising Catholic. It is somewhat startling to
recall, then, that the saints to whom we are referring had
already arrived at the height of their mystical life when they
received the stigmata; while that of Therese, on her own testimony and that of her director, had not yet begun. Therefore it
is here a permissible inference that the external wounds were
not an expression of the interior wound of love; in other
words—since we have no evidence, nor even a suggestion from
either Therese or her intimates, that there was present this
wounding of the soul by love—that the physical phenomena
had no observable relation to the condition of her soul. Thus,
the conclusion that Therese's stigmata are not a mystical grace
but a charisma suggests itself; and we have cited earlier on
Dom Mager's rather sceptical view of charismatic stigmatization. On the other hand, the absence of mystical contemplation at the time of the reception of the stigmata would seem
to strengthen the case of Poray-Madeyski, who considers it a
hysterical phenomenon.

We would now recall Mgr. Teodorowicz's contention that
although Therese had no mystical life at the time of her stigmatization, she developed it in consequence of this grace.
Though we know of no canonized saint in whose life the order
has thus been reversed, yet Almighty God is free to bestow His

[74] Teodorowicz, p. 161.

gifts as He pleases; hence the possibility of her developing a mystical life afterwards cannot be dismissed conclusively in advance.

The stigmata of Therese Neumann, then, show marked differences from those of the saints; they appeared during a period of severe physical and mental weakness; they were not given all at once, but appeared only gradually; and, thirdly, they were not preceded by a mystical life, that is, they were not the result of infused contemplation. They were, however, connected with visions, considered by Poray-Madeyski as hallucinations, and these visions will have to be examined next.

CHAPTER VI

Visions of the Passion

Accorning to her own account of her first visions on March 4th-5th, 1926, Therese saw Our Lord kneeling in the Garden of Gethsemane. "I saw all the other things, too," she says, "very distinctly: the trees, the rocks, everything as in a garden. And I saw three Apostles, but they were not lying down or sleeping, as they are usually pictured, but sat rather, leaning on stones, and were entirely powerless." [75]

There is one arresting feature in this account: it is that the disciples are not sleeping. In this it does not differ only from the usual pictures, but from the New Testament narrative itself: "And he cometh to his disciples, and findeth them asleep." [76] The salient feature here, that which makes the account so tragic, is precisely the fact that they were asleep. "What," Our Lord says, "could ye not watch with me one hour?" There is no mention of their being powerless, but precisely of their being asleep—asleep, while He was watching in His agony. It is noteworthy that Therese's vision omits this important point and substitutes instead the un-Scriptural statement that they "were entirely powerless"—which would have exonerated them from all fault and made Our Lord's reproach meaningless. It is therefore most difficult to subscribe to Teodorowicz's statement that "Theresa's visions are in full harmony with the Gospel truth," [77] an assertion contradicted more than once in future visions. For we have now to consider other visions of the Passion scenes which show equally incongruous characteristics. What is perhaps most surprising

[75] Von Lama, p. 47f.
[76] Matt. 26: 40, and parallels.
[77] Teodorowicz, p. 443.

is that Therese takes an active part in what she sees. We quote one remarkable account in Archbishop Teodorowicz's own words:

"But is Theresa merely an inactive observer of these terrible events that are taking place in Jerusalem? I behold her countenance and say to myself: 'No.' The greatest excitement shows itself on her face. Thrown into the midst of invisible, horrible events, *she is no inactive observer but one of the most spirited participators, one that would, through her participation, hinder the tragedy of Golgotha if possible*. . . . During the periods of rest, she breaks out with the words: 'We will lead Him home yet.' Surely, here she means the Saviour whom she hopes to save . . . She is no despairing, helpless witness of the terrible tragedy of Calvary, like the Mother of God,[78] the holy women or even the timid, fearful Apostles. She is personally active, a Joan of Arc in the presence of her Saviour. She does not fear the enemies of Christ, who are rejoicing over Him. She does not despair for a moment as to the success of her attempt to rescue Him. That she has formed a plan to save her Master through flight, that she has also brought assistance for the accomplishment of her plan of saving Him, is attested by her words, 'I know a shorter way.' She points out the road with her finger in the air, with all its turns and deviations, that she has before her eyes, and she repeats meanwhile: 'So, so and so.' Her decided tones reveal that she wants to enter into the minutest detail of carrying out her plan of safety for Christ."

The Archbishop continues: "Theresa's words, 'We wish to lead Him home,' reveal a mystery to us that is present to her unique consciousness. In the moment when Theresa speaks these words, there is no Cross for her, even as there is no crucified Saviour. How will He be crucified, whom she is to save through flight? The mere thought of His death sounds like blasphemy in her ears. While she was telling the pastor

[78] It seems strange that the Archbishop, in his admiration for Therese, should let himself be carried so far that he will call the Mother of God, whose title of Co-Redemptress may perhaps one day be officially proclaimed by the Church, "a despairing, helpless witness."

of the beams that the Saviour has to carry, he made the remark: 'The Saviour will surely be nailed to these beams.' To which she indignantly replied: 'How can you say such a thing? I will accuse you to the Saviour.'" [79]

It was the reading of this account that first caused the present writer to assume the cautious attitude maintained in these pages; and it seems worth while to analyze it in detail.

The most obvious point of interest in Teodorowicz's description is that the principal actor in the scenes of the Passion is— Therese herself. The rôle allotted to Our Lord in these visions is secondary; He appears to her not as the Son of God, redeeming the world and ruling from the Cross; not as the *Sanctus Deus, Sanctus fortis, Sanctus et immortalis* of the Good Friday Liturgy, but as a helpless victim evoking pity but no awe. There is no hint in these strange visions that Our Lord once called St. Peter "Satan" when the Prince of the Apostles tried to hinder him from fulfilling the purpose for which He had come into the world; nor of the fact that only a few hours before His Passion He had said to the same disciple: "Thinkest thou that I cannot ask my Father, and he will give me presently more than twelve thousand angels?" [80] But she does not witness these scenes which would give her the clue to a proper understanding of what follows. The folowing hypothesis, though of course not final, seems suggestive: she would not be able to assume her rôle of "a Joan of Arc in the presence of her Saviour" (the word "Saviour" is rather inappropriate in this context) if she knew the true significance of the events. For if she did, she would have been just another humble spectator like, say, St. Mary Magdalen.

But it may be objected that her desire to "save the Saviour" sprang not from ambition, but from love. If this is true, then this love here is the same purely human emotion that earned St. Peter the terrible rebuke: "Go behind me, Satan, thou art a scandal unto me, because thou savourest not the things that are of God. . . ." [81] It is hard to believe that visions which

[79] Teodorowicz, pp. 192f; italics mine.
[80] Matt. 26:53.
[81] Matt. 16:23.

come from God should inspire just such a desire to prevent
the Redemption as was so sternly condemned by Our Lord
Himself.

This absence of familiarity with the truths of the Faith displayed in the trances is very curious and, as far as we know,
unparalleled in the history of mystic experience. Teodorowicz,
however, cites St. John of the Cross as a witness to it. He
writes: " The obliteration of the memory that we come across
in Theresa Neumann cannot be regarded in the field of
pathology and psychology as a sick, somnambulistic condition
or a natural spiritual experience . . . St. John of the Cross tells
us that the operations of the soul in the unitive state proceed
from the Spirit of God and are of a divine nature. Concerning
the memory he says: ' The more nearly the memory attains to
union with God, the more do definite kinds of knowledge
become perfected within it, until it loses them entirely, namely,
when in perfection it attains to the state of union. And thus at
the beginning, when this is first taking place, the soul cannot
but fall into great oblivion with respect to all things, since
forms and kinds of knowledge are being erased from it.' " [82]

Teodorowicz concludes the quotation here, but St. John of
the Cross continues the discussion thus: " and therefore it is
guilty of many omissions in its behaviour and usage—forgetting
to eat or drink, and being uncertain if it has done this or no, if
it has seen this or no, if it has said this or no—through the
absorption of the memory in God." [83]   It is quite clear, therefore, that what the saint refers to here are the every-day occu-
pations that must ordinarily be retained by the memory if a
man is to lead a normal life, but which at a particular period of
the mystical life, namely, before a soul attains to the trans-
forming union, will temporarily be suspended in order to free
the memory from all things that prevent full union; above all,
as the Doctor of Divine Love never tires of saying: from just
such imaginary visions as Therese (i.e. on the assumption that
they are not hallucinations) would seem to have in her Passion

[82] Teodorowicz, p. 211.
[83] *Complete Works*, I, p. 229.

trances. For, writes the saint, "As God has no form or image that can be apprehended by the memory, it follows that when the memory is united with God . . . it remains without form and without figure, its imagination being lost and itself being absorbed in a supreme good, and in a great oblivion." [84]

What is so amazing in Therese's loss of memory during these trances is that she should forget precisely those things which one would expect to be remembered most when the soul is united with God, namely, the truths of the faith. It is the unanimous teaching of mystics and theologians that if God gives a soul *gratiae gratis datae* such as visions, or locutions, He illumines her understanding and kindles her love. [85] We observe in Therese, on the contrary, that her understanding is obscured rather than enlightened and that to such an extent that she does not even remember Our Lord's Divinity and what this entails. She knows nothing, as we have seen, of His omnipotence. Nor has she any recollection of His omniscience and His knowledge of the secrets of the heart; for how else can we explain her statement to Fr. Naber that she will accuse him to the Saviour?

We have already seen that in these visions her love for Our Lord is somewhat sentimental; and a lack of reverence seems to be manifested in a remark made during her state of exhaustion after a Good Friday trance: "Saviour, I have no time for you to talk to you now; I must sleep properly." [86] The saints, it is true, have sometimes permitted themselves familiarities with Our Lord from which ordinary Christians might shrink; but they have never crossed the border line beyond which familiarity becomes impertinence.

Another description, taken this time from the book of Ritter Von Lama, shows precisely the same characteristics. "Having forgotten completely all that had been learned—I repeat that I

---

[84] *ibid.,* p. 228.

[85] Cf. St. Teresa, *Interior Castle,* Sixth Mansion, Ch. 9; *Life,* Ch. 26; Poulain, *Grâces d'Oraison,* 20.39. "Les contrefaçons de l'imagination n'ont pas le pouvoir de développer ainsi nos connaissances"; Tanquerey, *The Spiritual Life,* p. 702.

[86] Gerlich, I, p. 125.

report only what I have personally observed—her sympathies
are extended to Pilate, who treated Our Lord with consideration; and even to Judas who gave Him a kiss. She does not, of
course, understand the Aramaic cry of the disciples, Galapa!
Galapa! (Traitor! Traitor!) and betrayal is not a visually repre-
sentable object, or was not, in this instance at least, so represented. She disapproves of Peter, whose sword-thrust caused
the first blood to flow. And when my guide (Professor Wutz)
interposed, ' Why, Resl, today you seem to be a bit stupid,' she
retorted quickly, ' And I believe you are even more stupid.' "

Von Lama continues: " Her utter ignorance of what is to
come is remarkable. After each succeeding separate ecstasy,
which at first last only a few minutes each, she is convinced
that Our Lord is to be set free, and she does not understand at
all when my guide tells her what must follow. She is under
the impression that Professor Wutz (who hears what she says
during the ecstasies) stands at the back of her, and that therefore she cannot see him during the vision. She said to him
when the cross-bearing Saviour had reached the outskirts of
the city, ' Hurry, now, to His Mother and tell her that they
have set Him free.' She insists upon this even after she had
been told by Professor Wutz that he has been told how the
people have planned to kill Jesus, and finally compromises by
saying, ' Well, tell her (the Mother of Christ) that Resl says
they will set Him free.' " [87]

We have here again, but in a new form, this remarkable lack
of acquaintance not only with the deeper meaning of what she
sees, but even with the rôles and characters of the persons
appearing to her. These curious conditions are discussed by
Teodorowicz. " A certain religious," he writes, " took umbrage
at Theresa Neumann's being favourably inclined toward Judas
when he kissed the Saviour because, according to St. John of
the Cross, God is supposed to teach the soul in ecstasy without
words, the soul thus grasping the teaching more deeply and
comprehensively. The entire objection shows a complete
ignorance of mystic teaching. Illumination and revelation in

[87] Von Lama, p. 124f.

the mystic state do not rest upon the increase of the natural knowledge but upon the arousing of the supernatural and thus cause love and interest for the divine mysteries. So the remark of St. John of the Cross about the teaching of the soul in ecstasy refers to supernatural knowledge. The soul can experience more deeply and comprehensively the mysteries of faith that draw it to divine love even if it lacks the knowledge of this or that tongue, even if it is not familiar with this or that historical scene. Theresa is illumined only in one direction that Christ suffers and that He suffers and dies for us." [88]

It is not certain that the " entire objection " of the unnamed religious (perhaps Dom Aloys Mager?) "shows a complete ignorance of mystic teaching." For the fact that Our Lord was betrayed by Judas is not merely a question of "natural knowledge" but is a truth guaranteed by the Holy Spirit in the Gospels, as is the fact that St. Peter is the rock upon which the Church is built, despite his precipitate action of drawing the sword in defence of Our Lord. These things are not just " this or that historical scene "; they are essential to our faith, proclaimed by the Church again and again in her Liturgy, and it seems strange, indeed, that the significance of just these scenes and of the personages involved in them should be completely hidden from the visionary of the Passion. On the other hand, not without difficulty can one agree that " Therese is illumined only in one direction, that Christ suffers and that He suffers and dies for us." The first part of the statement is correct; but if she is illumined on the fact that He dies for us, i.e. that His Death is the cause of our Redemption, why does she want to prevent it? If she were supernaturally enlightened on the significance of His Death, surely she would not wish to interfere with the events of the Passion by trying to lead Christ home, however much compassion (and surely she cannot have more compassion than Our Lady!) she might feel for Him.

In the account just cited she again takes action in a similar direction; she orders Professor Wutz to inform Our Lady that her Son will not die—in other words, that the Redemption will

[88] Teodorowicz, p. 463.

not take place. Can it therefore really be asserted that her illumination extends to the supreme redemptive value of Our Lord's suffering and death? Moreover, if there had been supernatural enlightenment, would not Therese have realized Our Lady's part in the Passion and that there was no need for the Mother of Sorrows to be informed about her Son's fate by "Resl"? It is the ineluctable fact that Therese's own person looms very large in these visions; how large is revealed in the following scene: "Only once in this ocean of pain," writes Teodorowicz, "does a soft, peaceful, clear smile float across her features. It must be something entirely conciliatory, something that she alone feels in this drama of suffering that causes it. The Saviour in this moment, with deadly tired but thankful and acknowledging eyes, looks upon her; and she smiles with exuberant joy of soul." [89]

There are, of course, several occasions in the lives of the saints when, in their visions, Our Lord thanks them for what they have done for Him. But we know of no example when this has happened in the middle of an "historical" scene presented to the imagination, indeed, in the supreme scene of the Crucifixion. In this hour it would seem appropriate that the visionary should thank Him rather than that He should thank her.

This impression is confirmed by Therese's own statement that what causes her the greatest pain is "that I am unable to help the Saviour." [90] The saints speak a different language. What causes them the greatest pain when contemplating the sufferings of Our Lord is not their inabiliy to help Him, who has all the angelic hosts at His command, but the conviction that they themselves have contributed to His sufferings by their sins. Before St. Gemma Galgani was stigmatized, for example, she felt a piercing sorrow for her sins and a particularly vivid sense of the sufferings of Our Lord—for, indeed, the two cannot but go together. Throughout the centuries of Christian experience the fruit of the contemplation of the Crucified has

[89] *ibid.*, p. 196.
[90] *ibid.*, p. 198.

always been intense contrition; and it is perhaps *the* most extra-ordinary feature in this extraordinary life that nowhere are we given any sign of the sinful lover's sense of personal guilt; nor is there any trace of the virtue of compunction. Therese, in all the available biographical material, never accuses herself of any faults; on the contrary, as we shall see in later chapters, she is always prepared to excuse and defend herself, while often accusing others. This absence of the *Mea culpa*—which, after all, is the most natural response of the Christian before his Crucified Lord—is extremely revealing, since Therese readily gives expression to her other feelings; thus, we cannot with complete justification attribute this absence to a natural reticence. What Our Lord wants of us, whether we be mystics, stigmatists or just " ordinary " Christians, is not a futile desire to " help " Him to come down from the Cross, which He could have done without our assistance had He so wished, but to make His Cross fruitful by acknowledging our sins that impelled His Love to die on it.

CHAPTER VII

Other Visions

UNTIL THE 6th of August, 1926, Therese had only visions of the Passion. But on this date a strange event took place. We relate it in the words of the person who seems to have caused it, viz. Professor Waldmann of Regensburg, whose generous help and interest have been acknowledged in the preface. This is his—hitherto unpublished—account:

My Experience at Konnersreuth on the 6th of August, 1926.

"On this Friday, which was at the same time the Feast of the Transfiguration of Christ on Mount Thabor, I went to Konnersreuth with great expectations. Till then, I knew, Therese Neumann had only seen the scenes of the Passion of Our Lord. But as a theologian, I said to myself: the Transfiguration of Christ is so intimately connected with His Passion that I should be surprised if, on this Friday, she would not first experience the Transfiguration, and only afterwards the Passion.

"During the whole train journey from Neustadt-Weiden, then my domicile, to Waldsassen, I talked about nothing else to my two fellow-travellers. My brother and I went from Waldsassen on foot to Konnersreuth and arrived at the house of the Neumanns about half past twelve in the afternoon. The room on the first floor was crowded with visitors, and so was half the staircase. There reigned complete silence. This I found surprising, for I had expected people to talk about the fact that Therese had seen something special today. I, too, did not talk.

"At last the clock of the parish church struck one. And presently I heard the voice of Fr. Naber through the closed door: 'Now all is over. Please will you leave the room so that it can be aired?' Thereupon the visitors walked out of the room, passing me on the narrow staircase, and those standing on the stairs followed. I myself, however, walked up the stairs, now empty of people, to the last step; in front of me was the closed door and a landing of about one metre and a half in breadth. I reflected. So Therese had not seen the Transfiguration. But I should be much surprised if the vision did not take place now. Anyway, I was not going to leave like the others, but remained. If the vision did not occur, well, then I would have a look at the Stigmata.

"This reflection of mine, which had hardly lasted a minute, was suddenly interrupted by the voice of Fr. Naber coming from behind the closed door: 'Quick, quick, run over to the Presbytery. The gentlemen should come back. Something new, entirely new!' There we are, I thought, the Transfiguration. And I entered the room at once, which had now been opened. Without mutual greetings (we know each other from our Seminary days) the Parish Priest hastened to call out to me: 'Look, look, Therese is seeing something extraordinarily beautiful, she is really as if transfigured.' To which I replied: 'Well, yes, Father, she is now seeing the Transfiguration on Mount Thabor.' With these words I stood in front of the bed, taking no notice of what was going on around me—the room had soon filled with people again—but concentrating wholly on what was happening before me.

"The body of the woman who was lying in front of me was as if it had become quite rigid, the upper part bent above the bedclothes in an angle of 45 degrees, arms and hands stretched forward and upwards, the eyes looking immovably in the same direction with an expression of contentment and joy. During the approximately three minutes that she remained in this rigid position I could not notice any breathing. Then, however, she sank back into the pillows and drew such an extraordinarily deep breath that I thought spontaneously: What a surprisingly healthy person; what lungs she must have! After about half a minute she sat up once more in her former rigid and immovable attitude without any noticeable change if compared with the first time. At this moment I announced in a loud voice, so that all present could hear, 'This will surely happen a third time.' The thought which was in my mind was this: in all probability she will see the Transfiguration in three scenes. I did not, however, reflect on the difference between the scenes in detail. Hence, she could not gain any information about this from me. And as I had announced, so it happened. She sank back into the pillows a second time, then raised herself up to the vision for a third time, and then sank back once more. Immediately afterwards I said: 'Well then, *now* it is over.' And without having looked at anyone, I walked away from the bed, left the room and went over to the Presbytery.

"I was profoundly convinced that Therese had now seen the Transfiguration. But had this vision been supernatural? Why, then, only now, and not *before* the visions of the Passion, as I had been expecting it for several days? Then I was thinking again: perhaps she has only now, like myself, been thinking of the Transfiguration and hence had the vision. I therefore asked in the Presbytery how Therese used to follow Holy Mass. I was told that she used the Prayer Book of Schott. Therefore I concluded that it was possible that she should have thought of it herself. A little later, Fr. Naber arrived and asked whether I did not want to have a look at the Stigmata. I said I would, and so we walked back to Therese, who was lying in a state of semiconsciousness. Fr. Naber touched one of her hands. She drew back a little, but when he said, 'It is I, the Father,' she quietly held out her hand for him. He removed the cover and I saw the Stigma: on the back of her hand there was a round mark the size of a halfpenny, covered with a diaphanous membrane through which one could see the blood. It was certainly not artificially produced. This I also said to the Parish Priest, but I added: 'Do not forget that theology has not yet solved the question in how far here, too, the principle should be applied: *Gratia supponit naturam.*'"

If this experience was already strange, the sequel is stranger still. The Professor continues:

"Already on the following Monday I received a foolscap

letter from one Fr. G.P. This contained roughly the following (the letter as well as the postcard to be mentioned later is with the Episcopal Acts of Regensburg): The letter writer remained at Konnersreuth during the night because he wanted to discuss pastoral affairs with Therese. For which he thanked God. For on the following Saturday at ten in the morning, Fr. Naber asked him to be present at the questioning of Therese on the subject of her vision of Friday afternoon. And there it appeared that Therese had not the slightest notion that on this day the Feast of Transfiguration had been celebrated. Therefore she had not quite understood what she had seen. She had thought it was the Risen Saviour, 'but He hasn't had anything,' meaning He had not had the Marks of the Wounds. But she has, continues the letter, actually seen the Transfiguration, and in three scenes, viz.:

" I. Jesus with three men on a mountain. Even the position is described in the letter: Jesus in the centre towards the front, the three Apostles behind Him, a little towards the side. Jesus and the Beloved Disciple were praying fervently, the two others less.

" II. Jesus transfigured in the clouds. 'Here it was that she did not know what was what. She saw the Saviour, but He did not have anything.'

" I was now looking for the third scene. But there was nothing in the letter on that. The whole third page is filled with thought about this new miracle worked on Therese, and the Divinely blessed diocese of Regensburg.

" I therefore wrote back at once, that I should be much interested to know what Therese had seen in this third scene. The answer came by postcard, bearing the date of August 11th: 'To supplement my letter. Therese has really seen the Transfiguration in three scenes. But I do not know how the third scene was distinguished from the second. *The persons were the same.*'

" Now I began to understand. Therese Neumann had only experienced something resembling the Transfiguration of Christ. She did not see Moses and Elias, nor did she see or hear anything of the conversation of these two with the Lord, nor did she hear the Voice from Heaven. Therefore she did not know what she had seen, thinking that she had seen the Risen Christ, though without the Marks of the Wounds. The Scripture knowledge of her school days had deserted her. From me she could read nothing except the subject of the visions. Hence her failure—but no trace of the supernatural.

"The suggestion of the vision, therefore, came from me. During her state of abstraction I was standing outside the door of the room, expecting the beginning of the vision very eagerly. She, however, read my thoughts and fulfilled my wish almost immediately. I am absolutely convinced that, if I had not come to Konnersreuth on that Friday, she would not have experienced the vision of the Transfiguration. And if I had already come on the Thursday, then she would first have seen the Transfiguration and afterwards the Passion, perhaps the Transfiguration also in three scenes, but with Moses and Elias and the Voice from Heaven. And maybe even in the manner in which Therese Neumann later, perhaps in 1927, told her biographer Witt her experience of August 6th, 1926. Here one sees quite clearly the alteration, colouring and embellishing of the experience with the assistance of Fr. Naber. The threefold division of the scene is no longer evident; it cannot even be read into the vision. Of course, Moses and Elias are no longer absent, as little as the Voice from Heaven, of which she said she understood nothing. Fr. Naber would have done better if he had not taken Fr. G. with him as a witness, and the latter, if he had not written to me. Thus, there stands now witness against witness, and obviously witness G's account is nearer the truth."

From this experience Professor Waldmann draws the following interesting conclusions:

"Therese Neumann's experience of August 6th, 1926, was a telepathic vision of the Transfiguration of Christ, occasioned by my eager expectation and brought about with the assistance of her reminiscences from her Scripture lessons. Actually, it can be indisputably seen from all reports about Konnersreuth that Therese Neumann, in the state of 'abstraction' in which she was on this Friday immediately after the visions of the Passion, is in telepathic relationship with her surroundings, especially with Fr. Naber, answering unformulated questions, knowing the state of health or of soul of persons, as well as relics, etc. All this, however, only on the presupposition that the persons present have a conscious or subconscious knowledge of these things. She therefore possesses telepathic faculties approximately to the same extent as Tertullian's Montanist ' Sister' mentioned in *De Anima* ch. 9, Catherine Filljung (1848–1915) and so many other spiritualist and scientific media. With *mere* hysteria, without parapsychological faculties, the riddle of Konnersreuth can therefore not be explained in all its details."

So far, Professor Waldmann. This experience, as well as its interpretation, of the learned Bavarian theologian throws new light on the case. It is now more difficult than ever to ascribe a supernatural origin to these events. No doubt hypotheses are not definitive proof, yet when they multiply so persistently and on such firm, logical and psychological grounds, one cannot help being impressed; their weight alone is convincing. At the same time it is noteworthy that though it is now accepted that Therese never has the Passion trances on great feasts and during their Octaves, even in Passion Tide (e.g., she did not have them on Passion Friday, 1948, which fell on St. Joseph's Feast, March 19th) the great Feast of the Transfiguration did not interfere with them.

Might it be suggested that this occurred because she did not *know* it was the Feast of the Transfiguration?

This, of course, does *not* mean that Therese *consciously* controls her trances. The appearance of this type of phenomena is produced by what psychologists call the "subconscious mind" as are, for example, our dreams. Applying this psychological datum to the case under consideration, we infer the following: Therese, in ordinary consciousness, knows there is a special feast on the coming Friday, hence she does not expect the Passion trances—her subliminal mind takes up this suggestion and actually fails to produce them.

Thus, according to Professor Waldmann, it is possible for Therese to reproduce visions by telepathy or suggestion. It may now be instructive to note the characteristics of visions that could have been thus induced and that are not connected with the Passion trances. We give a few examples.

"On December 23rd, Therese saw how Mary and Joseph resumed the journey at about 5:30 o'clock; how Mary walked at times to spare the animal and how she and Joseph became very tired, so that they prayed for help. They saw a house in the distance. The old man and old woman who lived there with their son and daughter welcomed the friendly strangers. They noticed our Lady's condition and how pale and tired she was . . . and gave up their meagre but warm meal to the travellers. Later Our Lord rewarded the hospitable old couple, for they died good deaths, heathens though they were. The boy grew up to hear John the Precursor preach and was baptised by him and then he became one of the seventy-two disciples of Christ. The girl became a Christian, too, and met death at the hands of the pagans when she tried to destroy their idols.

"The night between December 23 and 24," continues the account, "was spent by Mary and Joseph in a village inn. On December 24 they resumed the journey at 6 o'clock. The ass became tired in the afternoon, but people in a village along the route revived the animal with food without charging for it. The weather was cold and rainy. Therese saw how the holy pair reached Bethlehem about 5:45 p.m., entering by the northern gate . . . Mary and Joseph walked along to the stable guided by a lantern which Joseph had brought along. About 8 o'clock they reached the stable which was built on the eastern slope of a hill as an addition to a cave which formed its northern portion. The roof and wall were of wide boards, and in the wall to the right of the entrance was a small window. Joseph tied the ass to an upright beam in the farther left corner of the stable . . ." [91] and so on.

In another vision "she beholds the scene in the Temple where Peter cures the lame man. Happily and joyfully, the man wants to give Peter the money which he has in his hat.

[91] Schimberg, *The Story of Therese Neumann,* Milwaukee, 1947, p. 124f.

Peter refuses it . . . In the effervescence of his joy the healed man throws his hat into the air and the coins fall all around on the ground. 'But, Resl,' says one of those present, 'what a pity for the hat. I should like to have it.' 'You foolish man,' she answers, 'why do you want a hat that is all in tatters?'" [92]

Here the same features noticed in the discussion of the Passion visions are again evident. The visions are all concerned with physical and material details which frequently resemble those recorded in the apocryphal Gospels. Teodorowicz deals with the objection that "the images are not strictly historic, that many actually have legends for their background," and he replies: "But these pictures are not to replace geography or history; they are for the benefit and the salvation of souls." [93] There is no question at this point of the non-historicity of the visions; but there *is* question of the value of these visions with all their wealth of irrelevant detail for "the benefit and the salvation of souls." The very fact that the Church has rejected the apocryphal Gospels which ministered precisely to the instincts for the sensational that are present in these visions seems to us to be a reasonable argument against their supernatural origin. "The real purpose of these visions," Teodorowicz goes on to say, "is their reproduction of the celebrations and mysteries of the liturgical year." [94] But it is just the absence of the liturgical sense, as well as the quality of "mystery" that seems particularly characteristic of these visions, especially if compared, for example, with the splendid liturgical visions of a St. Gertrude. These, far from being occupied with unnecessary material details, go straight to the heart of the mystery they represent. They are "liturgical" and doctrinal and "mystical" in the truest sense of the words. The visions of Therese, on the other hand, are concerned with the earthly and material, however touchingly they may describe the "Butzerl" (Bavarian for "kiddie," her favourite designation of the Christ Child) and His surroundings.

Her visions from the lives of the Saints are less explicitly

[92] Teodorowicz, p. 447.
[93] *ibid.*, p. 452.
[94] *ibid.*, p. 453.

described in the books on her, and follow the Breviary accounts; they occur almost every day and are very brief. We
give one recounted in Poray-Madeyski:

"In another of her visions," he writes, "Therese contem-
plated the apparition of the Child Jesus to St. Anthony of
Padua. She saw the Saint extend his arms towards the Child
who descended towards him on a cloud, press Him on his heart
and cover His face with kisses. Therese asked him to give her
the Child for some moments, and when the Saint did not
answer she said to him: 'Wait, when He comes to me at
Christmas you shall not have Him either.'" [95] "You shall not
have him either"—a spontaneous and natural response that is
not easy to reconcile with a supernatural origin.[96]

---

[95] p. 85.

[96] Compare with these accounts what Fr. Gabriel, *Visions and Revelations in the Spiritual Life,* says about visions: "We may even say that
souls which cling to visions thereby hinder their faith from developing
and delay their progress on the way to union . . . Hence the first motive
for forbidding all affection for visions, all willingness to give them any
place of importance in our life, arises out of the very conditions of our
preparation for union with God. To be attached to visions, and to be
properly prepared for divine union are two incompatible states." (pp.
72, 73).

CHAPTER VIII

Publicity and Investigation

IT is hardly surprising that the events recorded in the preceding chapters should have aroused the curiosity of the
countryside surrounding Konnersreuth. Soon the journalists
of the local newspaper *Waldsassener Grenzzeitung* were on
the track, and on the 1st of April, 1926, Fr. Naber himself published a detailed account of Therese Neumann's cures and stigmatization in this paper—from which account his bishop, then
Dr. von Henle, received the first information of the marvels
that were happening in his diocese. Naturally enough, this
was " copy " and was soon taken up by newspapers and
periodicals throughout Germany and beyond, and the case of
Therese Neumann received a publicity far surpassing that of
other contemporary stigmatists, such as Padre Pio.

Public interest in Therese increased when, soon afterwards,
another phenomenon appeared: from the 6th of August, 1926—
incidentally the day on which she first experienced the vision
of the Transfiguration—she ceased almost completely to take
food, contenting herself with a little liquid each week. From
Christmas of the same year she gave up even that and was said
to take nothing except a spoonful of water with Holy Communion, on which from that time she is reported to be living.

When things had reached this point and the pilgrims to Konnersreuth increased in number, Bishop von Henle, who had
been opposed to the events from the beginning, ordered an
investigation, which was, however, limited to her inedia.* This
took place from the 14th to the 28th of July, 1927, not in a hospital as the authorities would have wished, but in her own
home. With the consent of her parents, Therese was subjected

* Prolonged fasting.

to a close supervision conducted by four trained Franciscan nursing sisters and under the control of Therese's doctor. During these weeks Therese had two attacks of vomiting mucus and blood and one nervous fit at night. The latter lasted twelve minutes, during which she hit out wildly, crying that something was stabbing her through the heart. This seizure was perhaps connected with an incident that had happened the previous evening. When Therese was in her "state of absorption," which ordinarily follows her visions of the Passion, the sisters had been talking to each other in whispers about the difficulties made for them by Therese's entourage. Therese suddenly began to sob and complained of terrible pains in her head and elsewhere. Then she seemed to listen to someone and presently declared that a "voice" had told her that her sufferings were due to the unworthiness of the four sisters who were betraying the great task with which they had been entrusted by cherishing unfavourable opinions of her and Fr. Naber. The sisters quickly apologized, whereupon Therese announced that the Saviour had forgiven them. Soon afterwards she went to sleep.[97]

During the fortnight's observation Therese led her normal life, going to church and for walks in the village. Only on Fridays did she keep to her bed. Her weight, which had been 55 kilo at the beginning of the period, fell to 51 kilo after the Friday trances and mounted to 54 kilo during the following days. After another temporary decline it reached 55 kilo at the end of the fortnight. The water was tested twice during this period, and its composition was found to be that of "hunger urine." During the two weeks following the observation by the sisters, water was sent in twice for examination, but its condition on these latter occasions was normal and showed no longer the chemical indications of hunger.[98]

This account, reproduced from Poray-Madeyski, shows curious features. The first is the evident reluctance of Therese and her family to comply with the request of the bishop, and

[97] Cf Poray-Madeyski, p. 68.
[98] Poray-Madeyski, p. 70.

the difficulties imposed on those charged with carrying out the unpleasant task of observation. This appears most strikingly in the "fit" she had during the examination. Where the saints are glad to suffer misrepresentation and humbly bear, or even rejoice in, the unfavourable opinion of others, Therese has a paroxysm. Further, a mysterious "voice," presumably Our Lord Himself, reveals to her the unworthiness of the sisters. Here again we are bound to note her readiness to accuse others and the habit of identifying her own views and feelings with those of Our Lord, which we shall meet again on later occasions. Far from reiterating the teaching He left us in the Gospels, that we should take upon us our cross and follow Him Who is meek and humble of heart, He is here represented as approving a natural indignation with those opposed to her. It is somewhat disconcerting to find that Therese invariably "comes out on top" in her visions and revelations; that no one is ever dissatisfied with her and that those who express criticism are usually rebuked. Only after the sisters have apologized to her is Therese able to announce Our Lord's forgiveness to the unfortunate nuns: a unique contrast to the behaviour of the saints who, however unequal in character and temperament, have in common that they prefer blame to praise, taking upon themselves the faults of others and suffering punishment though innocent of guilt.

The second puzzling feature in this account of the investigation of her inedia is that while her water showed the usual signs of a complete fast during the period of observation, it no longer did so when tested afterwards. All biographers are unanimous in mentioning Therese's absolute truthfulness. Yet we have seen in an earlier chapter that she was not above deceiving her mother about a physical weakness, and that she also deceived the doctor and sisters of the hospital at Waldsassen. These are indications certainly that her biographers have exceeded the evidence. We emphatically do not imply fully conscious, deliberate fraud. "If Theresa Neumann and her family," writes Teodorowicz, "falsely declare that she neither eats nor drinks, then for years in Konnersreuth a tremendous world fraud has been going on at the cost of truth, religion and the Church." [99] And he quotes Therese's own words, " ' Of what benefit would it be to my family to deceive the world and to tell them that I do not eat if in fact I do so secretly? Of what value would it be to us to plunge our souls into perdition through fraud and lies, through blasphemous confessions and communions? ' " [100]

Yet, in this matter of her inedia there is an explanation of the urinoscopic results that does not cast doubts on Therese's moral character. We shall later discuss the traits she shows of "split personality" and somnambulism. Here suffice it to say that just as somnambulists know nothing of their nocturnal excursions to the roof tops, etc., so Therese could have eaten in her trance state without having the least recollection in her waking state of having done so. But it may further be asked: how did she manage, then, to be entirely without food or drink for a whole fortnight; and how can food disappear in her house without any member of the family noticing it?

There are answers to these questions, too. We have already seen that during her illness, before there was any question of stigmatization, Therese had gradually lost all normal ability to take food, that she lived almost entirely on minute quantities of liquid. And so her fast, which has been continuing for over twenty years now, will in all probability be *almost* complete; though not quite, as the analysis of her water has shown. But there remains the complete fast during the fortnight of observation. We quote again Teodorowicz: "Before the Ordinary of Regensburg requested the Neumann family to give Theresa over to a scientific investigation, he asked sincere scientific circles about the necessary length of such an examination. The answer was that no one could last two weeks without eating or drinking . . . As long as exact science has not overthrown the former declaration of the experts in regard to the two-week examination, so long can we boldly assert that two weeks of abstinence from food and drink are amply suffi-

[99] Teodorowicz, p. 344.
[100] *ibid.*, p. 345.

cient to establish that Theresa Neumann's fasting is in no way naturally explainable." [101]

This conclusion, however, is not as decisive as it seems at first sight. It is true that scientists have not yet found a natural explanation for such a fast—but it is also true that there have been other instances of a *complete fast* (allowing not even for the infinitesimal nutritive value of the Host) *outside the Catholic Church.* Perhaps the most striking of these is the case of Mollie Fancher, discussed by Fr. Thurston in *The Month* of December, 1930, and January, 1931, which, even if it were the only case of a complete fast outside the Church (which it is not), renders untenable the opinion that a complete fast carried on for years must be of supernatural origin.

Mollie Fancher, a Protestant, was born in 1848 and lived in Brooklyn, New York. "For long years she was incapable of swallowing and lived almost completely without food, but in this crippled state she developed remarkable clairvoyant faculties." [102]   Fr. Thurston goes on to quote the testimony of a reliable witness who states that "the only nourishment she has retained in her stomach from April 4th, 1866, to October 27th has been four teaspoonfuls of milk punch, two of wine, one small piece of banana, and a small piece of cracker." [103]   Later the inability to retain solid food or drink seems to have become even more complete. "Water, the juices of fruits and other liquids have been introduced into her mouth, but scarcely any of them ever make their way into her stomach. So sensitive has this organ become that it will not retain anything. In the earlier part of her illness it collapsed so that by placing the hand in the cavity, her spinal column could be felt." [104]   Dr. Ormiston, her medical advisor, stated: "It seems incredible, but from everything I can learn, Mollie Fancher never eats." Dr. Speir, her doctor, said: "The case knocks the bottom out of all existing medical theses." [105]

[101] *ibid.,* pp. 337 and 340.
[102] *The Month,* 1930, p. 528.
[103] *ibid.,* p. 533.
[104] *ibid.,* p. 534.
[105] *ibid.*

Fr. Thurston continues: "In the presence of the facts just quoted it seems difficult to affirm with confidence that the disinclination for food which we find so constantly recurring in the case of almost all visionaries—Anna Catherine Emmerich, Domenica Lazzari, Louise Lateau, Therese Higginson, Therese Neumann, etc., not to speak of many canonized saints—is necessarily of supernatural origin." [106]

We can but subscribe to the view of the learned Jesuit: complete abstinence from food, however rare and extraordinary, cannot be adduced as a certain sign of supernatural intervention. This is also the view of Pope Benedict XIV who, after dealing with demonic feasts, writes, "*Colligitur ex dictis, longa jejunia duplicis esse generis, alia videlicet supra naturam, alia intra naturam.*" [107] Hence the statement of Archbishop Teodorowicz, "And so we stand before the grandiose phenomenon of the perpetual lack of food which, if solely and alone were proved to be true, would be able to raise the world out of its snares," [108] would seem somewhat exaggerated and open to contradiction.

Whatever, then, the outcome of the examination, whatever the length of the test or its efficiency, whether carried out in Therese Neumann's own home or in a hospital, the fact that she can live without food or drink is assuredly remarkable, but it is not proof for the supernatural origin of the other extraordinary phenomena in her life.

The effect of the positive result of the investigation, however, was tremendous. Professor Waldmann writes in a letter to me: "Now came the great days of Konnersreuth. Freiherr von Aretin, Dr. Gerlich, Chaplain Fahsel, Von Lama, Professor Wutz, began to form the 'Konnersreuth Circle.' There began a veritable migration to Konnersreuth. Both the Government and the bishop, and after his sudden death the Auxiliary Bishop Hierl and the Chapter, opposed the 'Konnersreuth Movement' and visits to Konnersreuth were forbidden. This was the situation when Dr. Buchberger came to Regensburg.

[106] *ibid.*, p. 535.
[107] *De Beatificatione*, IV, 1, 27; no. 13.
[108] p. 356.

In this context should be understood the Episcopal Commission as well as the criticisms by Professor Martini." It is this second investigation, which took place in 1928 (not, as p. 117 of Poray-Madeyski, in 1938) with which we have now to occupy ourselves.

It was conducted by the director of the University Hospital at Bonn, Professor Martini, in the presence of Mgr. Buchberger and several other ecclesiastical and medical authorities, in March, 1928. As the German original was inaccessible to us, we give extracts from the French translation, published in Poray-Madeyski's book.

On Thursday, March 22nd, Bishop Buchberger and the others came to the Neumanns' house. "Herr Neumann," writes Professor Martini, "asked to see the episcopal permit to visit his daughter, in order to show on this occasion that he complied with the orders of the Regensburg Ordinary (both father and mother conducted themselves as if they did not recognize the bishop); the father consents, however, to let the visitors enter after the bishop has assured him that he would be shown the permit later; he seemed reassured by the consent of the parish priest. We mount the stairs to Therese's room. She receives us, visibly somewhat embarrassed, but her manner remains frank and natural." [109]

After a little conversation the visitors return to the parents, who now receive the bishop as such. "In the course of the conversation that follows," continues Professor Martini, "the question comes up whether it will be necessary that Therese should once more be put under observation. The father, till then quite amiable, declares in an offended tone that he has already openly proclaimed that he would no more permit anything of the sort. He explains that after the fortnight's observation in 1927, he had been promised that that would be the first and last trial of the kind. He sticks to that. To the remark of the bishop that perhaps the Saviour Himself desires still more light on this matter he replies in a more moderate, but hardly more conciliatory tone." [110]

[109] Poray-Madeyski, p. 117.
[110] *ibid.*, p. 118.

There follows a very interesting description of the trances. When the bishop and his companions arrive, they have already begun.

"*The eyes are bleeding or are at least full of blood; but one cannot distinguish anything about the origin of the bleeding.*[111] The stigmata are not yet different from what they had been in the afternoon. Therese is in a sitting position, her arms extended horizontally in front of her. Soon her face becomes joyous. Fr. Naber explains that she is seeing angels. Soon afterwards she sinks back on to the pillows with a sorrowful expression, crying plaintively, 'Saviour,' and coughing. Fr. Naber turns her hand so that we can see the stigma in the palm of her left hand.

"Therese speaks of the moon. That there is a corner broken in the crescent. Killermann asks, on which side? She points to the left. Killermann explains that in the East the moon does not appear as she does with us, as a sickle, vertically, but horizontally, like a canoe. Fr. Naber hears that and insists with Therese whether it is not otherwise. Finally, to his pressing questions, Therese declares that the horn is missing, neither quite above nor quite by the side . . ."[112]

According to the information furnished by Professor Waldmann, Therese sees the moon as a sickle during the Agony in the Garden instead of a full moon, which would have been historically correct, because a picture of the scene hanging in the Neumanns' house depicts the moon as a sickle.

The report continues: "About 0:15 a.m. Always low sighs. According to Fr. Naber, about every fifteen minutes a small quantity of water is secreted, accompanied by lively pains. The mother confirms it. The mother has warmed the basin and passes it to her. Observation is naturally very incomplete. Therese speaks again: 'The crowd cries: Malada, malada!' She sees the crowd. 'The Saviour is now gone away.' Then, 'The Saviour comes back, so do I. The Saviour will not protest if I go away; the Saviour is good, better than all.' She

[111] This and following italics are those of the text.
[112] Poray-Madeyski, p. 118f.

then moans much that she is too hot and uncovers herself a good deal.

" 0:45 a.m. Killermann has touched her hand; she asks, 'Who is it?' and keeps worrying about it. No one except myself, not even the parish priest, has noticed the touch. Fr. Naber calms her, but evidently she has not succeeded in finding out who touched her. There follow disconnected words, clearly comprehensible, of a foreign sound: 'Magera, gallaba'; afterwards, 'coumé.' Fr. Naber translates this word by 'Rise' and ridicules Professor Ewald, who has attributed this word to the Upper-Palatinate dialect.[113] Then the Saviour says, 'Ana.' Fr. Naber explains at once, quite loud, 'It is I.'[114] Fr. Naber continues to comment, always rather loudly, the movements, gestures, and words which the young woman often pronounces in a very low voice; he affirms that at this moment she knows absolutely nothing of her ordinary life and ignores even that Konnersreuth exists. Fr. Naber turns the conversation to Judas. She affirms that he loved the Saviour much. Fr. Naber contests it, and a discussion arises between them . . . Therese . . . says some words aside to her mother, obviously intimating that she needs the basin; she sighs slightly. Fr. Naber explains, without us being able to understand the connection, that it is now the episode of the Mount of Olives. Therese sits up quickly. During this time, while complaining that she is too hot, Therese has lifted her cover two or three times so that one can see no more than her head. Behind the cover she makes movements with her arms and draws her leg up so that her knee appears on the left side of the bed and that her left foot hangs out.

" 1:05 a.m. *The wound of the left hand is covered with a little blood.* Therese calls often, 'Saviour. They have tied so tightly the hands of the Saviour; they have carried the Saviour so far; then there has been water: they have thrown him in

---

[113] Where it means "come" (H.C.G.).

[114] These comments of Fr. Naber should be kept in mind, since Archbishop Teodorowicz alleges that he knows no Aramaic and cannot influence her. See Chapter XIV.

and they have dragged him out backwards. His clothes are quite wet ' . . .

" 1:25 a.m. Killermann rises at the moment when she draws up her cover and tells me that now the wound of the heart is bleeding. I look at it, but believe that it is only a little blood put there from the wounds of the hands. At the moment when we turn round, both parents cry out: ' This is against modesty.' They themselves usually go out and did remain only today.

" 1:30 a.m. *On the left hand a streak of blood flows towards the wrist.*

" 1:45 a.m. Much sighing. ' I can no more,' is succeeded by, ' Saviour, Saviour.' And soon afterwards: ' You know how good He is.' In the region of the heart there appear now, too, spots of blood.

" 1:50 a.m. She is resting quietly on her back. Fr. Naber explains to us in a loud voice that she is in the ecstatic state of ' rest,' where she is perfectly happy. Therese then says to Fr. Naber: ' Now it is well.' And then, turning to us: ' Now there will be nothing more in particular till five o'clock.' Fr. Naber asks: ' Have you any pain? ' Therese: ' None at all.' Fr. Naber: ' You have visitors.' Therese: ' Do you know, the Saviour did not make me recognize the bishop, but I noticed it, nevertheless.' Therese says to one of the visitors that she has already once seen Killermann and Martini. Killermann tells her that she has never seen him till now, to which she replies that it is the Saviour who told her that. Therese says that within a week there would come to her a professor who seeks the Saviour and who would then become a Catholic, to-gether with his wife. To the question, ' How? ' she replies: ' By letter.' She then speaks of professors: science was for the most part incredulous. How does she know? The Saviour has told her so. Killermann: ' This is because for many people it is rather difficult to have faith.' Therese replies, ' Yes, because there is no humility.' To the question of Killermann: ' Does it give you peasure that the bishop has come? ' Therese re-plies: ' Yes, the Saviour is pleased.' One of the visitors says that there is also another important person. Therese seems not to know that he means the suffragan bishop and does not respond. Fr. Naber: 'Will there be today something the matter with the lungs?' (He seems to mean whether there will be a fit of suffocation.) Therese: 'Yes, in the afternoon.' Killermann contradicts her. Therese says that she ought to know, because 'the Saviour told her so.'

" 2:05 a.m. Fr. Naber affirms that Therese is asleep. Killermann contests it, and so do I, because I do not consider this state to be a natural sleep. Therese smiles and, addressing herself to Killermann, says: ' You, too, will believe it one day.' Killermann: ' That is pure imagination.' She is still smiling. Killermann speaks to her about it in a loud voice and asks whether one can call that somnambulism. Therese at once replies: ' No, it is not that.' And she asks us if we know what Socrates said. We ask her to tell us. Therese: ' He knew that he knew nothing.' Martini tells her that she, too, will one day be reckoned among the scholars. She gives no proper answer; she asks us: ' Do you know what is happening now?' And she continues herself: ' Now the Saviour is strengthening me.' Then she speaks about a Calvinist who has been with her several times and who believes firmly in her. To the questions whether she knows what Calvinism is, she gives no answer. To repeated questions she replies: 'You know it quite well yourselves.' Fr. Naber turns the conversation to the fact that Dr. Gerlich is a Calvinist. We speak about the reality of the extraordinary things that are happening to her. Therese: ' This you will not be able to decide. This will be revealed after my death.' Asked whether she will soon die, she replies in the negative, but rather vaguely . . . . The parish priest declares loudly that in this state she knows everything; if there is a row in the village that night, she can tell where it has been taking place and who was involved in it. She also knows who, in the Episcopal Chapter of Regensburg, is for or against her . . . ." [115]

The account continues after some irrelevant details:

" 2:58 a.m. Stoeckl comes.

" 3:05 a.m. We both must leave the room, she thinks. (That

[115] Poray-Madeyski, pp. 118–123.

means that she wants to relieve herself.) From outside we hear her sigh very much.

"3:10 a.m. *The wound on the left hand seems more full of blood. The face, too, is stained with fresh, moist blood.*

"3:30 a.m. The blood on the left hand has become dry.

"3:30 and 4 a.m. The blood on the left hand is still dry.

"8:35 a.m. *Much blood on the left hand. The face is completely covered with it. The headcloth is soaked with serosanguinolent.* Therese often sits up, the upper part of her body and her arms always in the same position. The expression of her face passes through various phases between pain and convulsion. When she lies down again, it takes on a calmer expression. She continues to sigh, 'Saviour. Saviour.'

"8:45 a.m. We must leave the room. Therese says that the Saviour wants to tell the Suffragan Bishop something.

"9:27 a.m. A Franciscan father is introduced. We re-enter with him (Killermann, Hilgenreiner, Martini and a Jesuit father). The Franciscan questions Therese in an apparently completely suggestive manner on a certain Father Weiss, a Franciscan who was stoned in Africa in the 17th century. Shortly after 9:30 Therese begins again to sigh, complains and wants some relief. 'Hot, hot, hot.' During this 'relief' she rummages about with something behind her covers which are once more piled in a heap.

"9:35 a.m. Therese has once more sat up, arms extended in front of her. Facial mimics as before. Bishop Buchberger has returned; he sees Therese and tells me that when he left (about 8:15) he noticed that *the headcloth had been absolutely clean.*

"*Remark:* The suffragan bishop Hierl reported in the afternoon that when he had entered the room at 8:25 in the morning, *this same headcloth was already completely soaked with blood.*

"11:10 a.m. Killermann is authorized to take a little blood on a piece of cotton-wool.[116] I test the pulse. It is full and good.

[116] Comment of Prof. Waldmann in a letter to me of 27 February,

"*c.* 11:30 a.m. The father or the parents complain that the air is bad. I go out with the bishop, but before that I observe that there is only dry blood on the left hand and also about the eyes. I ask Killermann and Hilgenreiner to make sure of this, and they notice it, too. I ask them to observe when and how the bleeding begins again. The bishop, on leaving, recommends that always at least one of the gentlemen should stay in the room.

"*Remark:* At noon Killermann and Hilgenreiner tell me that there was nothing to be done, that they both had to leave the room owing to the insistence of the mother. She told them that about this time Therese always needed at least one hour's complete rest, and that today, too, she must rest for some time quite alone. *When they returned, all was red with fresh blood.*

"Soon after 12 noon. I return with the bishop (Michael Buchberger). Therese remains now nearly all the time sitting up and utters from time to time plaintive little sighs; sometimes she wrings her hands, sometimes she holds them extended before her. Her face presents the same changes of expression as before, but, truth to tell, without more remarkable intensity. *During all this time the wounds do not bleed.*

"At 12:48 p.m., rather unexpectedly, a short rattle in her throat, then she suddenly sinks back on her pillows as if dead. I test her pulse, it is exactly the same as before. Then I go out. Soon afterwards . . . the Jesuit father recalls me urgently because Therese is supposed to have a fit of suffocation. I find Therese sitting up in bed supported by her father and Fr. Naber. Fr. Naber places a finger in her mouth, there comes out saliva and rather thick mucous. Therese is more calm for a moment, during which time there is no sign of suffocation, no rattles or cyanosis. Very soon another attack.

1949: "The observations of Professor Martini together with Mgr. Buchberger, Auxiliary Bishop Hierl, Dr. Killermann and the other gentlemen were and are, in my opinion, of the greatest importance for the historian of Konnersreuth. It seems certain to me that Therese's mother has ' helped ' with the ' bleeding.' Not only because of the observations of Prof. Martini and Prof. Killermann, but also because Dr. K. had the blood which he had removed examined, and it was found not to be ordinary, but menstruation blood."

I ask the father whether I may perform an auscultation of the back of Therese, who is once more sitting up. The father refuses very rudely. Fr. Naber much agitated, begins to justify this refusal: that would be dangerous; once already, when the sisters were there, she had almost been choked. The mother intervenes on the same lines. Fr. Naber cannot calm himself in his zeal of apology. The father proclaims that the Saviour is the only physician who can help. Fr. Naber insists that she herself has said that she has an obstruction of the lungs caused by phlegm (that means that any other diagnosis is superfluous). Then Therese, after having spat out rather than expectorated a little mucous some seconds later, has lain down again; she smiles and is evidently quite well; she presents no longer any visible signs of respiratory troubles; the father proclaims triumphantly that the Saviour has once more assisted her.

"Let us repeat once more: during the so-called attack of 'suffocation' there has been no objective sign of this, and especially *no trace of cyanosis;* on the other hand, the eyes were strongly turned upwards. The impression is absolutely one of an hysterical reaction." [117]

We have given this account of a medical expert at great length because it seems to us of the highest significance for an objective appreciation of the case and because we are not aware of its having hitherto been made accessible to the English-speaking public. No less interesting are the conclusions which the professor draws from his observations. He writes: "The fact that two or three times *the observers were removed just at the moment when evidently a new influx of blood covered the wounds arouses . . . the suspicion that during this time something happened that had to shun observation."* [118]

The doctor continues: "What I have heard Therese Neumann say, especially during the night of the 22nd to the 23rd of March, denotes an education much superior to that of a simple peasant woman of the Upper Palatinate . . . For the

[117] Poray-Madeyski, pp. 123–125.
[118] *ibid.*, p. 127.

just appreciation of her discourses, nothing seems so important
to me as Therese's own affirmation—if Fr. Naber has informed
us correctly—that all that she said during that night while in
ecstasy had been inspired by the Saviour Himself. If one
keeps this fact in mind we arrive at least at very peculiar
results. I am thinking here particularly of her conversation
with Professor Killermann as to whether she was suffering from
somnambulism, of the quite reliable statement of Fr. Naber
that in this state she can tell where there is a row in the village
and who takes part in it . . . and of Therese's question if we
knew what Socrates had said and her own reply to it. Should
all this be accepted as divinely inspired? " [119]

" Lastly," continues Professor Martini, " I see contradiction in
the course of the so-called attack of suffocation that happened
soon after 12:45 p.m., March 23rd. The thing itself would be
of no interest if the so-called fit had taken place without comments on the part of Therese . . . but Therese affirms to have
learned from the Saviour that in her state at the end of the
'ecstasy' what happened was an obstruction of the lungs
caused by phlegm which put her in danger of being suffocated.
A priori it is impossible to admit that such a state should
develop suddenly, which would have been the case with
Therese . . . Moreover, in the course of the attack itself one
could not perceive any of those heavy rattles habitual with persons who cannot expectorate save with great difficulty . . .
The whole gave me the impression of a voluntarily produced
spectacle, but with insufficient knowledge of the symptoms of
suffocation. However, I take good care not to determine up
to which point Therese is conscious of its being produced
voluntarily . . . But the question arises: how to explain that
the Saviour—as she pretends—should have given the young
woman medical information on her state—information, moreover, that strikingly contradicts the positive and quite evident
facts? " [120]

Professor Martini considers that there are especially two
points which require explanation:

[119] *ibid.*, p. 127f.
[120] *ibid.*, p. 128f.

" (*a*) There is, first, the violent intervention of the parents when I was trying to approach the bed of Therese with Professor Killermann while she was pretending to relieve herself, though at this moment she was not at all uncovered. However, this might perhaps be explained by exaggerated prudishness.

" (*b*) Then there is the action of the father making everybody leave the room under pretext of the air being too bad, of which there could be absolutely no question at the time . . . But what is especially apt to arouse suspicion is the fact that on these occasions all the visitors without exception had to leave the room, as was the case when the mother, in defiance of the desire of the bishop, which she knew, caused Professor Hilgenreiner and Professor Killermann to leave the room at about 11 a.m. The importance of the connection of this behaviour with the appearance of a new bleeding is surely evident. And it is in the same spirit of systematic obstruction of an exact observation that one must consider the violent protest of the father against auscultating his daughter during the crisis of suffocation.

"From this results: (1) I have not been able to find any proof of the spontaneous flow of blood from the skin, and (2) I have been struck by quite a series of facts which make it my duty to preserve a very critical attitude towards the phenomena.

"I am finding it extremely difficult to insinuate the possibility of a fraud in a case where certainly many people have drawn religious profit. Nevertheless, one has to reckon with this possibility. To make it psychologically intelligible one must remember that in the beginning of the occurrences Therese Neumann could hardly have been conscious of their effects in the near future. But when events were already taking their course it was too late to draw back, especially as not only her own and her family's honour were at stake, but— as she believes—also the honour of the Church and, what is not less important, the salvation of so many people to whom she had been of use spiritually, and to whom, in the case of a confession, she would do so great an injury. She might easily persuade herself that she had no longer the right to make such an avowal. One could suppose the same for the parents if from the beginning they had favoured some irregularity.

"I am myself in no way convinced that it is so. My reasoning only tries to make it clear that one cannot exclude the possibility of a 'pious fraud' on psychological grounds.

"One could object: And the parish priest of the place, who is her confessor? This objection is not conclusive, either; because one cannot say exactly up to which point Therese considers her activity in any way sinful because, according to her, they are pleasing to God and profitable for Jesus Christ and the Church, even if she 'helped' the phenomena a little in one way or another. In this respect one must take into account Therese's fundamental constitution, which is clearly hysterical, on which, especially after my conversation with Dr. Seidl, I have not the slightest doubt." [121] There follows a very important footnote, attributed by Poray-Madeyski to Professor Martini, but believed by Professor Waldmann [122] to be by Dr. Deutsch:

"As to the pretended readiness of Therese to let herself be transferred to a nursing home, one has to remember this: Therese affirms that the Saviour does not want at all that she should go into a hospital; however, she declares that she is willing to obey the bishop. The father says that he believes in the divine origin of the inspiration of his daughter. If the Saviour says that He is opposed to her being put under observation in a hospital, he has the right to obey the Saviour rather than the bishop. Thus, Therese can safely express her willingness to obey the bishop, knowing full well that owing to her assertion of the Saviour's opposition, her father will never give his consent." [123]

So far the investigation conducted by Professor Martini. In 1937, the bishop refused to authorize visits to Konnersreuth officially unless there was a very good reason.[124] The relevant

[121] Poray-Madeyski, pp. 129f.
[122] Letter to me of 27th Feb., 1949.
[123] Poray-Madeyski, p. 130.
[124] The present writer came to Konnersreuth with such an authorization, though no one demanded to see it.

notice in the *Amtsblatt fuer die Dioezese Regensburg* (Official Gazette for the Diocese of Regensburg) will be of interest in this connection.

"*Konnersreuth.* In the year 1927 Therese Neumann, on the order of the bishop, submitted to a fortnight's observation, supervised by her doctor, concerning her inedia. The account of this examination has been published. Since that time ten years have gone by, during which Th. N., according to her own statement, has partaken of neither food nor (for several years) drink. Doubts have repeatedly been voiced as to whether these statements are correct or are due to either deceit or delusion. The writings which partly affirmed and partly rejected the reliability of the statements of Therese Neumann cannot afford an ultimate clarification and certainty. The doubts and discussion can be finally settled only by another examination conducted and supervised by doctors; for the examination of the year 1927 could, it is true, state the facts as they then were, but could not furnish a confirmation or refutation of the alleged inedia during the subsequent years. Hence the bishop of the diocese repeatedly expressed the wish to the Neumann family to agree to such an examination. The whole Bavarian Episcopate (in 1932) and, under the date of August 4th, 1937, also the S.C.S. (Sacra Congregatio Sancti) Officii, concurred in this wish. Therese Neumann has, indeed, declared a readiness for such an examination, but her father has so far refused it or, respectively, demanded unacceptable conditions. In this state of affairs the ecclesiastical authorities can take no responsibility for the reality of the alleged inedia and for the character of other extraordinary happenings at Konnersreuth. Until, therefore, matters have been cleared up by another investigation, no more permits for visits to Therese Neumann are issued." In view of this ecclesiastical pronouncement, Teodorowicz's statement that "Theresa's father . . . does the best that he can and gives an almost heroic proof of his attachment to the Church"[125] sounds somewhat exaggerated.

[125] Teodorowicz, p. 355.

Apart from the obstruction of the wishes of the Ordinary (and even of the S.C.S. Officii), so evident in Professor Martini's account, what is perhaps most strange in it is the description of the actual happenings during the ecstasies. There is vivid facial mimicking, a few plaintive utterances and foreign-sounding words and, above all, the commentary of Fr. Naber who tells the audience in detail what Therese is supposed to see at any given moment in her visions. Then there is the disconcerting wealth of physical details: the need for relieving herself, fits of suffocation, manipulations behind the high German feather bed—very different indeed from the features of true ecstasy, during which all the needs of the lower nature are suspended while the body and such movements as it may be able to make (for example in levitation) are always seemly and dignified. So far as we know, the Church's mystics had no need to be handed bowls, nor did they require to have their rooms aired while in ecstasy, whereas, if the phenomena were of pathological origin, just such occurrences might be expected. The other features of this description tally with what we have noted elsewhere; criticism of others during her ecstatic utterances, and attributing to the Saviour all that comes into her mind during this state of trance. These characteristics will be seen to occur again and again in the following chapters.

CHAPTER IX

Clairvoyance and Hierognosis

A PART FROM the Passion trances and the fast, a feature that makes a great impression on her visitors is Therese's faculty of clairvoyance, i.e. knowledge of things distant. We give a few examples taken from Teodorowicz, disclaiming all responsibility for the accuracy of the facts reported; they are, more often than not, once or twice removed from the original source and thus difficult to verify.

"A convert," writes Teodorowicz, "who had made a general confession was reminded of sins in his life that he had forgotten to confess. 'When he received the Sacraments of Penance and the Eucharist for the first time,' Fahsel reports, 'he was called to Resl who was just then in the state of exalted rest. As he bent down to her, to his great surprise two sins of his past life were told to him. He had no longer remembered them . . . In that moment the unfortunate thought came to him that perhaps he had not made a good confession. But he heard from the lips of Theresa: 'Do not worry. Everything is forgiven, but you should know that everything is known.'" [126]

Another instance: "I myself," writes Teodorowicz, "was present at the following incident. Once, when only a few persons were in Therese's room, she was in a state of ecstatic vision. It was a Friday, about nine o'clock in the morning. Suddenly she began to complain loudly. To the pastor's question of what was wrong, she answered: 'An apostate has been here. He has denied the Saviour' . . . At that moment a priest came to us. He confirmed Theresa's words. Just

[126] Teodorowicz, p. 395f.

then a fallen-away priest, with whom we had come to Konnersreuth, had left the room.[127]

"'On Easter Monday,' says Fahsel, 'I was sitting with
Theresa. Suddenly she said: "Father, did a Mr. B. from
Lichterfelde-Ost ever visit you in Berlin?" I could not remember. Then she had someone hand her a thick memoran-
dum book and gave me the gentleman's exact address.'" [128]

"A nun in Marienbad who had learned that I was going to
Konnersreuth begged me to give a letter to Theresa Neumann . . . I handed the letter to Theresa while she was in the
state of abstraction. In a second, by merely touching it, she
grasped its contents. She drew far more from it than a person
would who had read the letter . . ." [129]

Two more cases that are significant:

"The first case was told to me by the priest who took part
in it. A man living in this priest's parish was at death's door.
The pastor had heard his confession, but was hesitant about
giving him viaticum because various signs seemed to point to
an unexpected recovery. Theresa was asked how much longer
he could live. Supported by her reply, the pastor believed
that he could postpone viaticum. Death set in unexpectedly,
and the pastor reproached himself for having asked Theresa.
He came to a conclusion about her that he did not make
public, namely that she was possessed with evil spirits since
her advice brought spiritual harm to a soul. This priest . . .
was called to Theresa when she was in ecstasy. And Theresa
told him what was going on in his soul. She gave him a clear
answer that was also a justification for the internal reproach
he had made against her." [130] There follows a circumstantial
story about the dead man's secret sins. As a punishment for
this, viaticum was not to be his in his dying hour.[131]

"The second case is that of a nun who had left her community and was leading a life in the world that . . . was caus-

[127] *ibid.*, p. 396.
[128] *ibid.*, p. 397.
[129] *ibid.*, p. 398.
[130] *ibid.*, p. 400.
[131] *ibid.*, p. 401.

ing scandal. Death surprised the former sister and she passed away without the sacraments. Her family asked Theresa about it and she, while in an ecstatic condition, answered that the one who had passed away was with the Saviour. The pastor was quite surprised at these words, and asked Theresa how she could say anything like that. Then Theresa summed up the entire spiritual life of the deceased . . . Theresa declared that this person always led a pure life, was always motivated by the best of intentions to serve God. The weak point in her soul was that in the exercise of virtue she always placed too much confidence in herself . . . In dying she received the grace of perfect contrition."

But Therese seems to have realized that this was not enough. Therefore she produced what was considered proof of the truth of her words. "She said to the pastor," continues Teodorowicz, "'That you may know that everything I am telling you is true, I now tell you there is a man coming here to Konnersreuth who is bringing several hundred marks in an envelope.' Then she mentioned the exact day of his arrival . . . The event took place as she foretold." [132]

One last example: "During an ecstasy she spoke of a fallen-away priest that she tried to excuse on certain grounds. He should not be condemned without further ado, because before his defection he was under the influence of another priest who, with all his uprightness, misunderstood his relation to ecclesiastical authority and always held up to the fallen one the alleged injustice of his superior. The spiritual authorities can err and judge a thing unjustly, but nevertheless obedience and submission is their due and one must be ready to make this sacrifice. None of us but the pastor knew who had counselled the fallen one, and the pastor at once recognized of whom she was speaking. He was most astonished at what Theresa had said because he had never attributed such a devastating influence, as she had announced, to this priest." [133]

Before attempting to analyze these remarkable cases we would first discuss the question whether similar phenomena

[132] *ibid.,* p. 401f.
[133] *ibid.,* p. 351.

have been observed in persons outside the Church, and in circumstances where diabolic interference seems unlikely. We base our remarks again on Fr. Thurston's studies in *The Month*. The reading of letters in sealed envelopes together with correct statements about the character of the writer is a phenomenon not infrequent among naturally clairvoyant persons. Fr. Thurston, in his article *The Knowledge of Things Distant,*[134] records the case of an illiterate servant girl, Emma, who used to perform such feats. In the same article he discusses the performances of the Polish clairvoyant, Stephan Ossowiecki. "It is noteworthy," he writes, "that in Mr. Ossowiecki's attempts to describe the contents of sealed envelopes, etc., he constantly furnishes details regarding the character of the writer or the circumstances under which they were written." [135]

An even more remarkable case is that of Mrs. Croad, born in England in 1840, of whom it is recorded that she told a thoroughly sceptical doctor a secret of his life; [136] like Theresa Neumann—and Mollie Fancher—she used to know what visitors were coming to see her long before they arrived. We mention these cases in order to show that clairvoyant faculties need not have a supernatural cause, making our own the view of Fr. Thurston, who replies to the question whether there exists such a thing as natural—accepting the word in its accustomed sense as opposed to diabolic or supernatural—clairvoyance: "I am strongly inclined to think so, though it must be confessed that we know absolutely nothing of the conditions which call it into play." [137]

We would submit that there are certain features in the examples given of Therese Neumann's clairvoyance which make a supernatural origin doubtful. It is with clairvoyance as with other similar phenomena: the most reliable test of their authenticity is the use to which they are put. Now, in the case of a Blessed Anna Maria Taigi and others who enjoyed this particular faculty, it was exercised solely for the purposes of

---

[134] *The Month,* Dec. 1926, pp. 481ff.
[135] *ibid.,* Dec., 1926, pp. 481ff.
[136] *ibid.,* Feb., 1931, p. 142.
[137] *ibid.,* Dec., 1926, p. 484.

charity and in obedience to a director or some person in authority.   It is noteworthy to remember that St. Gemma Galgani, for example, when she once ventured to foretell a visit from her confessor unnecessarily, was immediately rebuked by Our Lord, so that she never did it again.   For pride, or at least vanity, always latent in even the most saintly of Adam's fallen race, finds its nourishment only too easily in the display of such extraordinary gifts, which are therefore to be used only with the greatest circumspection.

In the first example cited from Teodorowicz's book there is a strange feature.   If it were necessary at all to remind the convert of his forgotten sins, we should have expected Therese to do so *before* he made his confession, so as to ensure the worthy reception of the Sacrament.   But why do it afterwards? Therese herself provides an answer: "But you should know that everything is known."   The question is: Known to whom? Surely no one would expect a Christian, let alone a newly instructed convert, to be ignorant of God's omniscience?   It seems improbable that Therese's knowledge of the two forgotten sins should be used as a proof of the fact that all things are known to God.   The only evidence given to the man is that his sins are known to Therese.   It appears that in this case there was no cogent reason for this display of knowledge—on the contrary, it disturbed the unfortunate man's peace of mind, which she had to restore as best she could.

The next example is even more disquieting.   For in the case of the apostate priest who had been visiting her, Therese made known the sins of her neighbour without proper justification. Moreover, she made no attempt to bring back the lost sheep, a reaction that has ever been that of the Saints.   She only " complained loudly " and displayed her knowledge of hidden things, without apparent need, since the priest in question was evidently not causing harm to anyone in the room.   The same criticisms apply to her revelation of the bad influence of one priest on another, recounted in our last example, with the addition here that error was attributed to ecclesiastical authorities. St. John of the Cross has some very severe words for those who make known the sins of others; and we will quote him without, however, meaning to suggest that Therese's knowledge is caused by the devil. "At times," writes the Saint, "the devil is accustomed to represent to the soul the sins of others, and evil consciences and evil souls, falsely but very vividly, and all this he does to harm the soul, trusting that it may spread abroad his revelations and that thus more sins may be committed, for which reason he fills the soul with zeal by making it believe that these revelations are granted it so that it may commend the persons concerned to God. Now, though it is true that God sometimes sets before holy souls the necessities of their neighbours . . . yet it is more often the devil who does this, and speaks falsely about it in order to cause infamy, sin and discouragement, whereof we have very great experience . . . Such knowledge as this, whether it be of God or no, can be of very little assistance to the progress of the soul on its journey to God, if the soul desire it and be attached to it; on the contrary, if it were not scrupulous in rejecting it, not only would it be hindered on its road, but it would even be greatly harmed and led far astray." [138]

St. John of the Cross here puts souls on their guard against trusting any revelations concerning the sins of others, particularly if they are accompanied by the temptation to make them known. In the case of Therese the incidents already related are no isolated instances. We hear, for example, that in passing a certain house she says to her companions: "Here much sin is committed." [139] Teodorowicz himself discusses this subject and excuses Therese by saying that she "does not know anything in her natural state of what she reveals to souls in her mystic state." [140]

Now, first of all, this cannot always apply, because it seems unlikely that she should have been in a trance while passing a house during a walk. Be this as it may, the excuse made by Teodorowicz seems to us to increase rather than to solve the difficulty. For it does nothing more nor less than relieve Therese of all responsibility for what she does or says in her

[138] *Complete Works*, I, Bk. 2, Ch. XXVI, 17, 18.
[139] Teodorowicz, p. 367.
[140] *ibid.*, p. 425.

"mystic state." If the Spirit enlightening her were really the Spirit of God, it would mean that during this state the Creator was taking away moral responsibility, and with it the freedom and human dignity of His creature, making it His irresponsible mouthpiece.

This interpretation is not so preposterous as it sounds. There have actually been devotees of Konnersreuth who have asserted that "Christ speaks through Therese Neumann,"[141] among them Chaplain Fahsel and Dr. Gerlich.[142] Though Teodorowicz himself protests with all desirable vigour against this view,[143] we cannot see that he voices a substantially different opinion a little further on when he writes: "She speaks as one who speaks in sleep. Hence she is not responsible for the words she speaks . . ."[144]

The question arises at once: if Therese Neumann is not responsible for the words she speaks in this state, who is? Teodorowicz goes on to say: "Theresa . . . does not consider herself a special organ through which the Saviour speaks. I scrupulously probed her about this. She has the deepest interior conviction that she does not speak of herself, but that she appears in this important rôle only for Him of whom she is merely a pliable tool in the hands of His higher will."[145]

This is not completely satisfactory. Either the Saviour speaks through Therese or He does not. If, as Teodorowicz says, He does not—how can she be "merely a pliable tool, in the hands of His higher will?" If Christ does not speak out of her, and if, on the other hand, she is not responsible for what she says in that particular state, who does speak and who is responsible? It seems to us that here we have got to the root of the matter, and we would endorse the opinion, which has been that of the late Dom Aloys Mager, that so long as the identity of the "Voice" speaking out of Therese Neumann

---

[141] *ibid.*, p. 247.
[142] *ibid.*
[143] *ibid.*
[144] *ibid.*, p. 421. Compare with this the trance utterances of the heretical Montanist prophetesses, discussed in Chapter 12.
[145] *ibid.*, p. 422.

when in this " mystic state " has not been investigated, no final judgment is possible on her case.[146]

There is also another consideration which justifies caution. In the case of the saints, their prophecies and revelations were always made in the state of full consciousness. When directing others and laying bare the secrets of their souls, they knew what they were saying and took full responsibility for their words and their effect. Teodorowicz himself cites Poulain's words that, " A true revelation may subsequently be altered involuntarily by the person who receives it." [147]   He goes on to say: " The possibility is also present of pointing out and explaining true revelation falsely. Is this possibility also present for the Konnersreuth revelations? Some people claim the privilege of infallibility for Konnersreuth. But according to my opinion, not with full right . . . *In Theresa Neumann the possibility of error is limited to a minimum,* but nevertheless not altogether excluded . . ." [148]   It should be noted that these words refer to a person not yet dead, a person whose case is the subject of deep and widespread discussion and much grave disapproval on the part of many serious theologians.

The very fact that she is unconscious of what she says, hence not in a position to take responsibility, must cause consternation; because this would mean in the first place that a person receiving a revelation would be less than human—a mere instrument in the hands of the power speaking through her; and secondly, that an error—which even Teodorowicz admits might be possible—would have to be attributed to God, which is absurd. We cannot have it both ways. Either Therese is liable to error, in which circumstance she is responsible for what she says; or else she is not responsible, which should mean, then, that *if* the spirit speaking out of her is the Divine Spirit, whether through the agency of good angels or directly, she ought to be infallible. This is also the view of Tanquerey, who gives three possible sources of error in private revelations: " failings in the human subject, wrong interpretation, alteration

[146] For this whole question see Chapter on " Mystic States."
[147] Teodorowicz, p. 418.
[148] *ibid.*, p. 419; italics mine.

by the seer." [149]   Therese does make questionable statements
while in the "mystic state." The story of the man who did not
receive viaticum because of Therese's apparently equivocal
reply is a case in point. It is not a question of Therese's responsibility for the unfortunate result of her words—under
these circumstances it is evidently the duty of a priest to follow
the line of action prescribed by the laws of the Church and not
to credit private revelations from however holy a person they
may come.[150]   But we do find the explanations when she is
confronted with the consequences rather puzzling. In order
to justify her statements, she reveals once again the secret sins
of another person, an act contrary, as we have seen, to the
prudent course suggested by John of the Cross in the passage
cited before. Though the priest in question is stated to have
learned later that Therese's allegations on the former subject
were true, this cannot be held to prove her prior revelation,
viz., that God desired to withhold viaticum from the dying
man. It is improbable that Divine Providence should have
employed means so obviously compromising and prejudicial to
Therese herself. However, it may be suggested that this
strange revelation was meant for her humiliation; if so, this
was not Therese's interpretation, for she immediately undertook to justify herself.

The next example deals with an almost exactly opposite
situation. Here we are concerned with a nun who had left
her convent and subsequently caused scandal, who died without the sacraments. Therese, however, says that she is with
the Saviour, and in order to authenticate her statement she
proceeds to give such an account of the interior state of the
sister's soul as would have made immediate entry into Heaven
possible. Therese ventures to give a proof of this essentially
unverifiable assertion by telling Fr. Naber that her statements
would be demonstrated by the fulfillment of a prediction con-

[149] A. Tanquerey, S.S., D.D., *The Spiritual Life*, p. 707f.
[150] Cf. St. John of the Cross, *Complete Works* I, p. 165, "I consider, however, that the desire to know things by supernatural means is
much worse than the desire for other spiritual favours pertaining to the
senses; for I cannot see how the soul that desires them can fail to com-
mit, at the least, venial sin, however good may be its aims . . . and
he that bids the soul desire them, and consents to it, sins likewise."

cerning a man who would arrive at Konnersreuth with a specified sum of money. It is logically false to infer the truth of
one assertion from the truth of another where there exists no
necessary connection between the two; and we question
whether such knowledge as this, which is, as we have seen, in
the power of many mediums, can be accepted as proof of her
knowledge of the state of souls in the next world.

But in this particular case, Therese apparently realized that
she had made a serious mistake and therefore tried to save her
reputation by the proof from telepathy. For Teodorowicz says
nothing about the real story of the ex-nun, nor about the ecclesiastical censures which she had incurred; a knowledge of
these reveals the story in an entirely different light. I owe the
complete details to Professor Waldmann. He writes: " In the
diocesan gazette of the archdiocese of Freiburg i. Br. appeared
the following notice (No. 23, Saturday, 20th Sept., 1919):
' *Excommunication.* The Most Reverend Archbishop has
placed the following persons under excommunication, for
grievous outrage committed against the Most Holy Sacrament
of the Altar, and for encouraging superstitious and sacrilegious
religious practices: 1, the Priest Josef Abel of the Missionaries
of the Sacred Heart of Jesus, Bavarian citizen; 2, the Priest
Kaspar Hutter of Waldburg in Wuerttemberg; 3, Maria Anna
Licht, spinster, known as Sister Canisia of Daxlanden. Where
necessary this punishment is to be published from the pulpit,
and the faithful are to be urged not to consort with the above-
named persons.' "

According to Professor Waldmann, Maria Anna Licht was a
simple peasant girl who had entered the Community of the
Sisters of St. Canisius at Fribourg, Switzerland, and later had
been dismissed. In the archdiocese of Freiburg in Baden she
became the centre of a pseudo-mystical circle, together with
the two priests named in the notice. She believed that a new
way of worshipping the Blessed Sacrament had been revealed
to her. The priests sent her consecrated Hosts *by post,* and
she arranged Eucharistic processions through the house in
which a great number of her friends joined; after these she dis-
tributed Holy Communion. She and her companions are said
to have placed the consecrated Hosts on their bare breast in

order to induce ecstasies . . . Since, at last, Canisia had become pregnant by one of the priests, she prophesied that the child would become the Second Redeemer; if people did not believe her, the French would invade the country (1917–1918). The Redeemer, however, turned out to be a girl.

This Sister Canisia died at Moersen in the archdiocese of Freiburg in the year 1923 without having been reconciled; hence did not receive Christian burial. On April 4th, 1929, one Frau Eich from Neuburgweiler, and a Fraeulein Licht from Daxlanden came to Konnersreuth. They showed Therese Neumann a photograph of "Sister Canisia," and after the ecstasy received the information from Fr. Naber: "Canisia went to Heaven immediately after her death." On May 16th, 1929, the Freiburg archiepiscopal authorities applied to Regensburg for confirmation of these facts; the parish of Konnersreuth stated on July 4th, 1929, that these reports were true.

From this it would seem that the very fact of Therese's eagerness to prove the truth of her revelation does not tell in her favour. Confirmation of this found in Teodorowicz who writes that, "Where she is convinced that there is no honest attitude to the Konnersreuth events, she becomes stern and hard, inexorably hard, to those who doubt as well as those who believe in these happenings. She treats such people with repugnance." [151] Whereas the saints leave it to God to vindicate them, Therese does so herself; throughout her life we find an expression of this attachment to her special graces, and persons who have "no honest attitude" to them are treated "with repugnance."

In addition to the form of clairvoyance just treated there is another one called "hierognosis" (i.e., the recognition of sacred objects), also frequently met with in stigmatics, which Therese is said to possess in a high degree. "Her biographers," writes Poray-Madeyski, "give on this subject a series of very striking cases. The correctness of the information she gives in this matter has often been extolled; it has, however, been contested more than once." [152] Thus, her stigmata cause her

[151] Teodorowicz, p. 40.
[152] Poray-Madeyski, p. 99.

lively pains as soon as they are touched with particles from the
True Cross or other relics of the Passion. In July, 1930, for
example, a Capuchin Father touched one of her hands, which
rested on the wound of the side, with a reliquary. At once she
became as pale as a corpse and sank back on her pillows. The
Capuchin explained that the reliquary contained a particle of
the Cross, whose authenticity had been doubted. Fr. Naber
now declared the relic to be authentic. "However," continues Poray-Madeyski, "it is not only if touched with relics
of the Passion that Therese's stigmata react in this way. The
same painful reaction is produced at the contact of a piece of
linen soaked in the blood of Therese's own stigmata or of those
of another stigmatized person."[153] Poray-Madeyski then gives
an example of this same reaction of Therese's stigmata when
touched with a piece of linen containing blood from the stigmata of Louise Lateau. "Therese began at once to tremble
and to sob; then her complaints became almost shrieks of pain,
which ceased only when the little bag (with the linen) was
removed from her hand. According to the comment of Fr.
Naber—who repeated what Therese had said about it in the
morning—this experience proved that the blood from the stigmata of Louise Lateau was authentic, and that all the events
of Bois d'Haine were true and trustworthy. 'Louise Lateau,'
she said, 'went to heaven immediately after her death, without passing through Purgatory.'[154] We believe," continues
Poray-Madeyski, "that if one applied the deductions made
by Fr. Naber in this case to other cases of similar reactions of
Therese Neumann, as do several other persons of the 'Circle
of Konnersreuth,' one might come to conclusions which would
go beyond the limits of discretion necessary in this matter.
According to an account of Von Lama, Therese, in her state
of absorption, reacted to the contact with an image of the
Sacred Heart of Mirebeau, bearing the pretended marks of
blood, in the same way as she reacts to the touch of true relics
of the Passion. This image (of the Sacred Heart of Mirebeau)
had been given to Fr. Naber by the Counsellor Boeller, of

[153] Poray-Madeyski, p. 100
[154] *ibid.*, p. 101, cited from Von Lama.

Gladbach; Therese had not been informed of its origin. As soon as the parish priest, in the presence of the Canon of Bamberg Cathedral, Mgr. Geiger, and Therese's father, had applied the image to her heart wound, she began to sigh and complain: 'Dear Saviour, you pierce me, you burn me so much.' Then Mgr. Geiger interrogated her on the subject of the Abbé Vachère (author of the legend of Mirebeau), 'Tell me, Resl, where is the Abbé Vachère now?' 'In heaven, with the dear Saviour,' she answered. 'But how can he be, seeing that, because of his disobedience, he was excommunicated by the holy Pope Pius X, and died impenitent?' objected Mgr. Geiger. 'He is in heaven; he was innocent,' said Therese; 'he was a pious priest; one has been deceived in him; the gentlemen have done wrong; the Saviour was satisfied with his conduct.'"[155] This incident speaks for itself; we would only remark that it seems somewhat difficult to reconcile with "her deep appreciation of subjection to ecclesiastical authority" that "particularly touched" Archbishop Teodorowicz,[156] and is often praised by other biographers.[157] Therese's knowledge of sacred things is by no means so infallible as is claimed. Rather we find that if proved wrong she attributes error to the highest ecclesiastical authorities. One may not presume to judge where only the Church is competent, but surely it is proper to note once again the contrast that exists between these revelations and those of such saints as Teresa of Avila, Margaret Mary, or Joan of Arc.

[155] *ibid.*, p. 101ff. The most important words of this statement are in the original German: "Man hat sich an ihm geirrt, die Herren haben falsch getan."

[156] Teodorowicz, p. 351.

[157] Cf. Fr. Gabriel of St. Mary Magdalene, O.D.C., *Visions and Revelations in the Spiritual Life*, p. 33: "There is no need to confuse the 'mystic' with the 'visionary.' Certainly not with the false visionary, deluded by his imagination and obstinate in his own opinion! It is a fact that often deluded souls do not allow themselves to be moved in the least by those who are trying to lead them back to sound reason. Fully convinced of their relations with God, they can no longer obey even the ecclesiastical authority. Just think! The idea of contradicting communications that have been heard from the lips of God himself! How rash! The fact is that their follies often throw discredit not only upon revelations but upon the mystical life itself."

CHAPTER X

Other Phenomena

A PARTICULARLY interesting characteristic of Therese's trances is the frequent prediction in one of what will happen in the next. Here are a few examples recorded by Archbishop Teodorowicz.

"One thing that was striking to me in the mystic states of Theresa Neumann," he writes, "was the prediction of the ecstasies during the state of exalted rest.[158] The hour and the moment or general facts which exactly and punctually took place at the time specified were foretold. Thus, in my presence during an ecstasy she foretold that at eleven o'clock in the forenoon she would be in the state of exalted rest, and . . . this prediction was literally verified. She likewise predicted in the morning that she would have an evening vision ecstasy of the Transfiguration of Christ on Mount Thabor, and actually at the stroke of nine this same began." [159]   Another case is given in the words of Fr. Fahsel. "On the day of this event, July 25, 1930, Father Haertl stood near Theresa Neumann, who was in the state of exalted rest, and he heard her say: 'Tomorrow there will be a little excitement; but it does not need to be burned.' The surprised priest, who felt that something extraordinary would happen to Theresa, and that he bore responsibility for it, asked her if he and the pastor would be present. And she replied: 'You will be called.' This mysterious direction was illumined by the following experience. As the priest was leaving the schoolhouse on Saturday evening, the pastor, all excited, met him and asked him to go to Theresa with him

---

[158] On her various " states " see Chapter 12.
[159] Teodorowicz, p. 265f.

because she had to vomit the Host.[160]   The pastor's perplexity
was increased by the attitude of ' Resl,' for she knew nothing
of the remark of yesterday.   She lay there helpless and be-
moaned the event and prayed.   The only alternative for the
pastor seemed to be to burn the consecrated Host.[161]   Only
Father Haertl remembered Theresa's words of yesterday:
' It need not be burned.'   And thus it happened.   Theresa
swallowed the Host which the pastor handed her on a
handkerchief." [162]   After some remarks on the impossibility
of a medium making such announcements, Teodorowicz continues: " It should be added that all announcements of
Theresa about her coming ecstasies are as a rule made after she
has received holy communion, in answer to the pastor's questions. This circumstance made a particular impression on me.
The moment of the reception of holy communion . . . seems
to me to be the least fitting in which to be occupied with the
ego, even if with the best intentions." [163]   So the Archbishop
sought for a possible explanation, which he found in the idea of
a " mystic secretariate." " There exists," he writes, " a sort of
invisible but reliable secretariate in ecstatic stigmatization.
One of the duties of this secretariate is to protect the stigmatist
from all exterior accidents that might befall her, when, for
instance, those around her are unaware of the moment when
the ecstasy may set in.   The ecstasies come very suddenly and
overcome the stigmatist.   It might be disastrous if she went
into an ecstasy in the street or when in the company of
others." [164]

This is an ingenious explanation, but not quite in keeping
with the facts of history.   Perhaps there may be accounts of
mystical experience that would support this hypothesis, but we

[160] Presumably she had received Holy Communion in the afternoon,
which is possible for her because she takes no food.

[161] This would seem to be an error.   Theologians recommend that if
the sacred species are intact, the Host is dissolved in water and then
disposed of; only if it is impossible to distinguish it in the regurgitated
matter is burning the proper procedure.

[162] Teodorowicz, p. 270.

[163] *ibid.*, p. 271.

[164] *ibid.*, p. 272.

can recall no case in which ecstatics were protected in this
manner. On the contrary, their ecstasies frequently happen in
circumstances far from favourable. We need only think of
St. Catherine of Siena, who was thrown upon the rubbish heap
by angry lay brothers to finish her ecstasies unprotected in the
blazing sunshine; or of Blessed Anna Maria Taigi, who was
overtaken by ecstasy among her pots and pans or at dinner,
only to be sneered at by her infuriated husband. Far from
making things pleasant for His chosen ones, Almighty God
seems ordinarily to give these outstanding graces in the most
difficult and apparently uncongenial circumstances, destined to
humiliate and embarrass those who receive them.

There is, however, another case quite similar to that of
Therese Neumann, recorded by Fr. Thurston in *The
Month*.[165] Marie-Julie Jahenny, who was also stigmatized,
made frequent announcements on future developments in her
state, predicting new forms of her wounds, etc., and everything
always took place exactly as she foretold. Fr. Thurston discusses various possibilities of explanation, excluding conscious
fraud, which seemed in that case as unlikely as in the case of
Therese. " What alternative explanation is left us? " he asks.
" Are we to say that Marie-Julie was a saint stupendously
favoured by God? or a soul for the time being, at any rate, held
in bondage by the devil? or simply a religiously obsessed
neurotic girl, so phenomenally suggestible that the ideas latent
in her subconscious mind had the power to work out their own
fulfilment even in her physical frame? I must confess that it
is the last solution which seems to me, both in this and in other
similar cases, to accord best with the verifiable data." [166]
"There is also reason to suspect," writes Fr. Thurston, " that her
religious spirit was not such as we are accustomed to associate
with the idea of high sanctity. The canonized saints in almost
every known case were anxious to hide what they believed to
be God's supernatural favours . . . Marie-Julie, on the other
hand, seemed distinctly to court publicity, and the announcements made in her ecstasies of future developments seem to

---

[165] March, 1931, pp. 234ff.
[166] *The Month*, March, 1931, p. 240.

have been the reflex of this habitual attitude of her sub-conscious mind." [167]

Of the two explanations of Archbishop Teodorowicz and Fr. Thurston, that of the latter seems for the case of Therese Neumann to be more plausible. There is a distinctly sensational flavour about these announcements; especially in the last case, of the vomited Host. That it was necessary for the Host to be ejected is serious enough in itself; disposing of It would have been the ordinary procedure in such cases—But why should the incident be foretold in this peculiar way? "To-morrow there will be a little excitement"—these words, we are told, were Therese's words. And they seem to fit the case.

But if Teodorowicz's explanation of the "mystical secretariate" be unacceptable, there remains the other consideration which had struck the Archbishop himself—that just at the moment when one would expect Therese to be most absorbed in Our Lord, she speaks of herself and the phenomena that are going to appear. Other strange happenings that accompany her Communions from time to time seem to be in line with Fr. Thurston's interpretation just quoted. We give some examples from Teodorowicz.

"An eyewitness," the Archbishop writes, "described the following incident to me. Theresa was staying in his home during some family difficulties, and while there undertook expiatory sufferings for the dying mother of some well-known scholar. Her physical and spiritual sufferings were terrible. But how great was his surprise when Theresa suddenly in an ecstasy opened her mouth, her hands folded on her breast, then closed her mouth and bowed her head just like someone who had received Holy Communion. The surprise and the shock of the one who is my authority in this affair, the head of this house, reached its height when he found that the conse-crated Host that had been intended for Theresa was missing in the house chapel. The same witness told me an analogous, if not more surprising, case. Theresa was in Konnersreuth, several hours by rail distant from the place where he was.

[167] *ibid.*, p. 243.

One day when the pastor brought her Holy Communion, she was already in the state in which she usually is after communion. Theresa told him without any further explanation that she had already received on that day. In the meantime, the priest who told me the story noted that on the same day and at the same hour one of the three consecrated Hosts that he had reserved in his private chapel had disappeared.[168]

"Another similar thing," continues Teodorowicz, "was told me by the pastor. But since Fahsel actually took part in the event and minutely describes it, I will make use of his account. 'On Friday, June 26, 1931, Theresa came to the rectory at half-past ten. She looked wretched and apparently felt weak. We discovered that she had previously been suffering for a dying person. She asked the pastor to give her Holy Communion. She had received the day before. I went over to the sacristy. Theresa had taken the sacristy key with her but was too weak to open the door. We locked the door behind us and Theresa weakly stumbled into her chair behind the altar . . . While the pastor, kneeling on the step, was saying the Confiteor, I took the ciborium out of the tabernacle. After saying the two prayers, I went round the left side of the altar to Theresa's chair while the pastor went round to the right. When I was about a meter distant from her and raised the sacred Host to say the last prayers, I noticed to my astonishment that she did not turn to me but sat quietly in the chair facing the back of the tabernacle. It was the same position that she always takes while in the state of exalted rest after receiving Communion . . . Just then she began to move. She turned to me with eyes closed, raised her head somewhat and opened her mouth. There I saw lying on her tongue a white shining Host.' [169]

"We know from the history of the saints that there are precedents in these cases of miraculous Communions. Teodorowicz himself adduces that of St. Catherine of Siena. There is, however, a marked difference between the few instances of miraculous Communions recorded in the lives of the saints and

those of Therese Neumann. St. Catherine and other saints
received Holy Communion miraculously when, for some reason
or other, they were constantly refused this consolation by the
priests. In the case of Therese the priests were perfectly ready
to communicate her; in the last instance the priest was in fact
already standing before her with the Host in his hand. It is a
principle of theology that God does not accomplish by a
miracle what can be done in the ordinary way by secondary
causes. If, as in the case of St. Catherine for example, the
secondary causes, that is to say here the priests, refuse to
operate, then God may deign to work a miracle for His friends.
But it seems very improbable that He should do so when there
is a proper agent quite prepared to do the work. The whole
scene—Theresa stumbling into the church at half past ten in
the morning (rather than attending Mass at the customary
time) too weak even to open the door, receiving without the
ministrations of the priest, putting out her tongue in order to
show that there is actually a Host there—savours a little of the
dramatic. Fr. Thurston, recounting a similar story of Marie-
Julie Jahenny, who first opened her mouth to show that no
Host was there and after that opened it again with a Host lying
on her tongue, makes the following comment: 'The suggestion
of a conjuring trick in which the performer takes off his coat
to show that there is nothing up his sleeve is irresistible.' [170]
But he continues: 'It must be remembered that these things,
happening during trance, do not by any means imply that
there was a deliberate and conscious act of deception. But
they probably reflect a certain insincerity and self-centeredness
in the subliminal mind, and it is not easy to suppose that they
could happen in the case of one to whom God was all and herself nothing." [171]

So far as can be determined from the circumstances, as well
as from the evidence available, these miraculous Communions
are both unnecessary and too sensational to demand a supernatural explanation; whereas the interpretation of Fr. Thurston
fits all the circumstances without casting aspersions on the

[170] *The Month*, March, 1931, p. 244.
[171] *ibid.*, p. 245.

moral character of the subject beyond the denial of a high degree of perfection. Stories of the disappearance of Hosts from distant Tabernacles have been told of many " stigmatics," among others of the notorious Palma, of whom Pope Pius IX is reported to have said: ". . . . her pretended miraculous Communions with Hosts taken from St. Peter's are a pure piece of trickery. It is all imposture, and I have the proofs there in the drawer of my bureau. She has befooled a whole crowd of pious and credulous souls." [172] Certainly there is no question of *conscious* trickery in the present case, nor of demonic possession whose characteristics are entirely different; but we would submit that where such strange phenomena abound, great caution is always needed. It is only too easy to rest one's faith on such apparently " miraculous " events and to be more deeply shocked than is good for one's spiritual balance if what had been thought to be the immediate action of God turns out to be no more than an abnormal psychological phenomenon. The Church in her wisdom sets her children a most striking example in this respect; she canonizes heroic virtue but not extraordinary phenomena, of which procedure there is perhaps no more striking example than St. Thérèse of Lisieux, from whose earthly life extraordinary phenomena are so conspicuously absent.

The same remarks would seem to apply to another curious feature of Therese Neumann's trances, viz., her alleged knowledge of languages that she does not know in her ordinary state, to which Archbishop Teodorowicz devotes a whole chapter of his book. After referring to the Pentecostal gift of tongues, the Archbishop claims that, " In Theresa Neumann the charisma of speech has developed to a greater extent than is the usual case of the stigmatists.[173] Theresa," he continues, " speaks not only Aramaic, which was spoken at the time of Christ, but, as she also has other visions besides that of the passion and they are always accompanied by words, she speaks that language which is appropriate to the period of the scene viewed. How many words she uses is beside the point, for

[172] Cited in *The Month*, Oct., 1919, p. 299f.
[173] Teodorowicz, p. 470.

she is not giving a language lesson." [174] But the question of
the number of words used is not altogether beside the point.
For it is easier to retain few words of a foreign language in
one's memory than a large number. And as we shall see,
Therese's vocabulary of the foreign languages she hears in her
trances is very limited. We give some examples of languages
other than Aramaic. In a vision of St. John coming out alive
from the cauldron of boiling oil she remembers the words of
his prayer: " *Jesus Christos, Theou hyios, ego bios.*" (Jesus
Christ, Son of God, I am the life.) [175]

Now this is an extremely interesting phrase. For in the whole
New Testament the term *bios* is used only five times: once in
St. Luke, twice in the Pastoral Epistles, once in I Peter and
once in I John. *It is never used metaphorically,* but always
either for "life" in the literal sense or with a derogative meaning, as in the First Epistle of St. John in the phrase, "the pride
of life." Wherever the life of the soul, Christ as the Life, etc.,
is meant, the word *zoe* is invariably used. In the Gospel of
St. John, *zoe* (*bios* does not occur in it at all) is used in this
sense no less than 34 times. Are we really to believe that the
author of The Fourth Gospel suddenly used the term *bios* with
its distinctly literal or pejorative sense in place of the ordinary
metaphorical term *zoe* constantly used in his Gospel? Or is it
not more likely that somebody with an insufficient knowledge
of New Testament Greek made up this sentence and suggested
it, perhaps telepathically, to Therese as fitting in with the
emphasis of St. John's Gospel on Christ as the Life? We do
not think that any New Testament scholar would accept this
example (the only Greek one that has come to our knowledge)
as evidence of a supernaturally produced knowledge of Greek.

"Modern languages," write Teodorowicz, "are spoken by
her, too . . . She recognises Portuguese by its sound. Father
Greve relates how ' in the reception room in Konnersreuth on
July 16, 1928, the Bishop of Petrolina, Brazil, was waiting.'
Father Greve was telling him in Portuguese about Theresa's
stigmata. Unexpectedly she was heard to say: ' It seems to me

[174] *ibid.*, p. 470.
[175] *ibid.*, p. 472.

I heard that language in the ecstasy.' This time, I thought, she must be mistaken . . . Bishop Lisowski and I were conversing about the extraordinary events in the life of the stigmatist without paying particular attention to Theresa. She suddenly interrupted and assured us with childlike ingenuousness, but very insistent, that she did hear this language in her vision. Then Father Naber took part and said that if Theresa was not mistaken, then the only time she could have heard any Portuguese in vision would have been on June 13th of the previous year. She had had a vision at that time on the Feast of St. Anthony of the great wonder-worker of Lisbon making a visit to a noble friend at his castle, that had taken place 700 years previous." [176]

Too much in this account is vague. Therese asserts that she had heard that language, but obviously neither remembering when—Fr. Naber had to intervene with a suggestion—nor understanding what was said, simply affirming that she recognised the sound. A particularly interesting feature of the account is that she interrupts a conversation between two bishops in order to inform them that she had heard the language they were speaking in a previous vision, even insisting that this was so when opposed.

More impressive than the words she reproduces from other languages is her knowledge of Aramaic. Over this there has been considerable controversy. Now, a first point to be noted is that extremely little is known of this language; a second, that whatever she hears in her visions, she cannot, of course, repeat in a linguistically correct form. Hence it seems a somewhat hasty statement to assert that "Theresa Neumann speaks the colloquial Aramaic which differs in many respects from the language reconstructed by scholars." [177] Since no one knows what "colloquial Aramaic" was like, it is hardly possible to affirm that this is the language Therese hears and reproduces.

There are also other difficulties. Poray-Madeyski writes: "In her state of 'absorption,' Therese possesses a certain aptitude to retain and repeat according to their sound words and

[176] *ibid.*, p. 472f.
[177] *ibid.*, p. 477.

phrases in foreign languages heard in the course of her visions. It seems, however, that this aptitude has developed in her only gradually. At first she was not able to remember or repeat even the last words of Our Lord on the Cross; it was only after Professor Wutz (an expert in Semitic languages) had quoted to her the words in several languages, among others in Aramaic, that she recognised these last as authentic. (Note that a telepathic connection between her and Professor Wutz would suffice to explain the recognition, H.C.G.) By the same procedure Professor Wutz helped Therese to recognise the words of the angel Gabriel to the Blessed Virgin at the moment of the Annunciation, by citing them in Aramaic, according to the text of the Gospel." [178] Poray-Madeyski adds in a footnote the following statement from the biography of Witt: "But Therese could not repeat the words of the foreign language; she had not been able to remember them after hearing them only once . . . Nor could she say the words . . . Only in the course of time became her memory capable of remembering some of the things she had heard." [179] After this it is somewhat difficult to share the indignation of Teodorowicz with Professor Ewald, whom he quotes as writing: "Unfortunate from a scientific viewpoint, it seems to me, is the influence of another priest (viz., Professor Wutz), whom I do not wish to deny does it in good faith, but who visits her very frequently and in his high-spirited manner has without any doubt drummed a good deal into her. Thus, and only thus, can it be explained that Theresa has of a sudden begun to hallucinate in Aramaic, while formerly the Saviour's words were given by her in good Upper Palatinate . . ." [180] The Archbishop objects: "Three words are amply sufficient to overcome all doubt that Theresa is not externally influenced in her knowledge of Aramaic, and that in this particular case she absolutely cannot be making use of German words that were translated into Aramaic for her. These words that are not found in the Gospel are the expression of the incensed and

[178] Poray-Madeyski, p. 87f.
[179] Cited by Poray-Madeyski, p. 88, from Witt, II, p. 11.
[180] Teodorowicz, p. 479.

excited Apostles over the treachery of Judas. They are:
'Magera, baisebna, gannaba.' [181] . . . Professor Wutz cannot
be regarded as the originator of these words because they
were unknown to him and he did not know or understand their
meaning." [182]   But if Professor Wutz did not know them, how
can we be sure that they are Aramaic? I do not know
Aramaic, but I know a little of the Upper Palatinate dialect; and
these words sound to me suspiciously Bavarian (I do not know
whether Teodorowicz who, I believe, is Armenian by birth,
knows the Bavarian dialect). The explanation that " Magera "
is a borrowed word from the Greek *machaira,* sword, is ingenious—but could it not also be the German word for thin, which
is *mager? Baisebna* could be *Baiser Bua,* i.e., bad fellow, and
gannaba sounds very much like *Gang aba,* go away. There is
no more convincing reason to suppose that these words are
Aramaic rather than Bavarian. It is, as every linguist will
admit, extremely difficult to make conclusive statements about
an almost completely unknown dead language; and in Therese
Neumann's Aramaic there may well be a good many words
made up in her trance state that resemble known Aramaic
words, and which experts like Professor Wutz are trying to
puzzle out. Within the scope of a dead tongue there is more
freedom for such improvisation than in a living one. This is
probably the reason why Therese's French is limited to words
such as " Mon Dieu " or " Sche sui la Conceptiune Immacu-
lada," [183] whereas she is much more " fluent " in Aramaic.

A final consideration that would seem to make the supernatural origin of her linguistic ability at best doubtful concerns
Therese's own attitude to it. We have already seen that she
does not conceal the gift. On the contrary, she evidently
attaches great importance to it: " She can," says Teodorowicz,
" persistently battle about every Aramaic letter," [184]   Once the
Archbishop asked her " if it were not possible that Professor

[181] *ibid.,* p. 480.

[182] *ibid.*

[183] Teodorowicz, p. 473.   He thinks the latter quotation an exact reproduction of St. Bernadette's dialect—might they not equally well be a
mixture of badly pronounced Latin and French?

[184] *ibid.,* p. 9.

Wutz had suggested the Aramaic words and phrases to her.
' Oh, never,' she answered, ' that would have been impossible.
I only say what I hear during the ecstasy and I did it long
before Professor Wutz ever came to Konnersreuth. You see,
when I heard the strange tongue it was unpleasant for me
just as it is for anyone who hears a language that he would like
to understand and does not get a word of it. And therefore I
complained that the Saviour speaks a language that I do not
understand at all. But no one paid any attention to it. Professor Wutz was the first that questioned me about the
language. He wanted me to repeat the words that I had
heard. And I did it.' " [185] But even with Professor Wutz
she had to find fault occasionally. "That is," writes Teodorowicz, "what happened to Professor Wutz, who questioned
Theresa very thoroughly about Aramaic. She afterwards said
to me about him: ' This priest knows this foolish tongue well
(she meant Aramaic) but he is a very inquisitive priest.' Then
she turned with the words: ' You must look upon the Saviour
and not be so inquisitive.' And turning to the Saviour, she
said of the Professor: ' He means well, but he is too inquisitive.
He ought to gaze upon You.' " [186]

According to Teodorowicz, the question has been asked as
to what is the purpose of these phenomena of speech. He
answers that, " In Theresa Neumann the charisma of speech
has a far-seeing, double purpose. On the one hand, it completely enhances the visions with which it is most intimately
united and, on the other, it is an exceptionally strong proof for
the supernatural character of her visions on the whole." [187]
The cogency of these conclusions cannot be admitted without
reserve. The usual criterion of theologians in regard to the
supernatural character of a vision is its effect on the soul of
the recipient: if it increases humility, charity and other virtues,
it can with reasonable assurance be attributed to God; if it
does not do that, no number of other phenomena, however
strange or extraordinary, will prove its supernatural character.

[185] *ibid.*, p. 486.
[186] *ibid.*, p. 461.
[187] *ibid.*, p. 489f.

Teodorowicz attempts to justify the supernatural nature of the "speech charisma" from St. Paul. Though admitting that the Apostle does not set great store by it, he continues: "However, he (i.e., St. Paul) acknowledged and sanctioned the supernatural value and the importance of the speech charisma," [188] and he quotes I Cor. 14: 2, 9, etc. But it appears more likely that the Apostle here is referring to a very different phenomenon, not to the Pentecostal gift of tongues, i.e., the speaking of the Apostles in languages that they did not know but which enabled their hearers to understand them, but to the ecstatic, incomprehensible utterances *en vogue* especially in Corinth, which no one could understand, except those who had a special gift for interpreting them. But it is not this kind of speech that Therese hears and reproduces; hence, St. Paul's words do not necessarily apply to her.

There are innumerable experiences in Therese's life of a similar order, so many, indeed, that to examine each one in detail, as has been done with those above, would exceed the scope of the present study. I would refer the reader for these to Archbishop Teodorowicz's book; it is comprehensive and thoroughly documented. Throughout I have selected what I consider to be the most significant incidents for analysis, hoping thereby to indicate that *everything* concerned with this case is not above question.

[188] *ibid.*, p. 489.

CHAPTER XI

Expiatory Sufferings

IN THE lounge of the inn where I was staying during my days at Konnersreuth I met a garrulous old man who offered to tell me all about Therese Neumann, and who enlarged particularly on her expiatory sufferings, the famous "Suehneleiden," as they are called in German. With awe in his voice he told me how she suffered almost every day for sinners, souls in Purgatory and the dying. "She's had another *Suehneleiden* this morning"—which seemed to be a frequent occurrence in her life. The first of these, the alleged cure of a seminarist, is given great publicity in the popular biographies. Now, just this cure has been carefully investigated by Professor Waldmann, who had the kindness to put his material at my disposal. Here is the account he has sent to me, in which, "because of the delicacy of the case, the names of those concerned have been omitted. Original documents are with the episcopal acts."

"In June, 1931," the professor writes, "I received the book by Dorsaz-Lama, *Konnersreuth* (Waldsassen, 1931), for examination for the purpose of the Imprimatur. In the French original I found the tale of the candidate of Theology, afflicted with throat trouble, about which there had already been much talk. 'A candidate of theology,' runs the account, 'had been taken ill with such serious throat trouble that the Bishop refused to ordain him. Therese heard of it, had pity on him and took over his illness. In consequence, she herself became so ill with a paralysis of the deglutition muscles (November, 1922) that she had to consult the doctor, and from that time she could no longer take any solid food, not even Holy Communion. Only from the Feast of the Epiphany, 1923, she was once more able to swallow at least a small fragment of the Host. The theologian, however, so it is said, had been miracuously healed of his throat trouble.'

" This 'miracle' I resolved to investigate. Within a few days I was in possession of the material, according to which the first and original candidate for the miracle was a priest of the Ordination course, 1927. Owing to a communication from Fr. Naber this priest was questioned in November, 1927, in a letter from the President of the Bavarian organization of Catholic Priests and asked what he had to say about this allegation. He, however, rejected the notion of a miracle having been worked on him with so much vigour that he had to be counted out. Now Therese herself was asked in the 'state of elevated rest,' and lo and behold, a new candidate for the miracle was found who, however, had still been at school in 1927 and who only now, June, 1931, was about to be ordained.

" Though he was just making his Ordination Retreat, I went to see him. The question embarrassed him, for fear of Fr. Naber and the Konnersreuth Circle. He came from the parish of Konnersreuth; but nobody had ever been at pains to interrogate him on the subject of the miracle. Since the publication of the book of Gerlich (1929) he knew that the 'miracle' would be laid at his door, but was obviously afraid of protesting against it. This second theologian, too, however, denied as definitely as the first that a miracle had happened to his person. In order to escape possible embarrassments and unpleasantness, he celebrated his first Holy Mass not in his home parish, but very quietly at Regensburg. And not at 6.30, as was planned at first, but neither at 9, as Fr. Naber puzzled it out, but at 8 o'clock, because the seminary choir was dispensed from their ordinary duties for this one hour.

" And now let us compare what the literature on Konnersreuth has to say about this ' double miracle ' of the cure of the candidate of his throat affliction and of that of Therese Neumann of her paralysis of the deglutition muscles! In the tale of her biographer, Witt (in *Konnersreuth im Lichte der Religion und Wissenschaft*, 1927, pp. 54ff.), the normal Therese knows as yet nothing of a mystification of her throat trouble. 'Already, since 1922,' she says, 'I have hardly been able to eat anything. My throat trouble appeared for the first time at the end of December, round about Christmas. For twelve days I have not been able to swallow even one drop . . .' (At the same time her biographer significantly remarks on p. 56 'that during the interruptions of the visions on Friday he has observed repeatedly quite normal movements of swallowing in Therese.' Consequently: hysterical paralysis.) The mystification began only in 1927, probably occasioned by the First Mass of another new priest from Konnersreuth, whose Mass was served by the first candidate for the miracle. The responsibility for this miracle tale rests probably with the friends and relatives of Therese, that for the second obviously with Fr. Naber and the trance personality of Therese, who gave the information according to his expectations but—was mistaken, both on the candidate for the miracle and on the hour of the Mass. With this should be compared as a *non plus ultra* the presentation of the event by Therese Neumann, Fr. Naber, and Teodorowicz."

We now supplement Professor Waldmann's account by citing the event as reproduced in the book of Teodorowicz:

"I visited Konnersreuth in July, 1931, and was to give Theresa Holy Communion. I was prepared to give her only a small particle of the Host. But the pastor told me that now she could receive an entire particle. I said in surprise: 'And how about her throat? For years she could not swallow an entire Host.' 'Yes,' replied the pastor, 'but just yesterday (June 30) the throat pains ceased completely.' He explained the whole affair to me. From words of Theresa that she spoke during the time of exalted rest, those around her knew that she would be suffering from the throat affliction for him for whom she was suffering until he had been ordained and had said his first Mass. Here mention must be made that Theresa does not wish to know what she says in the state of exalted rest, a wish scrupulously obeyed by the persons about her. But the date and even the hour at which the first Mass was to be said were noted. It was to take place on June 31 (*sic*) at

Regensburg at half-past six. Should Theresa's prediction
come true, then on this day at seven o'clock in the morning
she should be freed of her throat trouble. These expectations,
however, went awry. The suffering did not cease but became
so much worse that Theresa could hardly speak. Three hours
later the pains suddenly and completely ceased. Theresa felt
entirely recovered. The throat was healed. What had happened? Because of some unforeseen circumstance the first
Mass was delayed from half-past six until nine o'clock (compare Professor Waldmann's remarks on the real time of the
Mass). At about half-past nine the consecration took place.
At the same minute Theresa was healed." [189]   These two
accounts, one from a critical investigator on the spot, the other
from hearsay, speak for themselves. They will serve to make
possible a more correct appreciation of the stories of similar
cases that are to follow.

Here are a few examples of them, taken from various
sources. " Theresa," writes Archbishop Teodorowicz, " freed
her father from a severe intestinal trouble through her vicarious suffering. This was told me by Professor Wutz of Eich-
staett, who, while riding in an auto with some of the family,
said to Theresa: ' You could actually take upon yourself the
sufferings of your father that were bothering him so?' ' Yes,'
answered Theresa. ' And I almost had to laugh,' said the
professor, ' when almost at the same moment a loud rumbling
was heard in Theresa's intestines. This was a symptom of
Mr. Neumann's illness.' " [190]

According to Von Lama, cited by Poray-Madeyski, " About
the middle of January, 1930, Theresa had influenza and a grave
pneumonia with a temperature of 103 degrees, in order to
merit the grace of repentance for a dying young girl from the
Rhineland. The unhappy young woman was the daughter of
a farmer, who had been seduced by an apostate priest at the
age of fourteen. Her parents were deeply Christian; their
child, who had lost the faith, was dying. Theresa suffered
her sufferings; she was tortured by a burning thirst, but as

[189] Teodorowicz, p. 369f.
[190] *ibid.*, p. 368.

soon as she was brought any refreshment she refused it merci-
lessly. In addition, she was very feverish and had incessant
violent temptations, so that she needed the assistance of the
priest, without which she would have succumbed." [191]

She also suffers for souls in Purgatory. "When Therese has
suffered for the deliverance of a soul from Purgatory, this
soul, according to her, comes as soon as she has been delivered
to speak to her and thank her." [192] But we are told comparatively little about these sufferings. As Teodorowicz rightly
remarks, "All exact checking of this suffering and vision is
out of the question.[193] We are only informed that she suffers,
for example, thirst for a drunkard, or worries about material
things for a miser." [194]

It is significant that what is apparently the same story as the
one of the seduced girl cited above is given in a considerably
elaborated form by Teodorowicz, who tells it according to the
account of Fr. Naber. We have here the same feature met
with in the beginning of this chapter, namely, a certain
unreliability of the written sources on these particular phenomena of expiatory sufferings.

There are other doubtful features. "If the persons," writes
Teodorowicz, "are unknown to her, the sufferings of these
persons are also unknown. Yet she suffers exactly the same
thing as the persons in question, whether it is pneumonia,
dropsy, blood-poisoning or some other malady." [195] But, we
may ask, if the persons and their diseases are unknown, how
does Therese know that she is suffering for anyone in particular? The answer is: because Our Lord tells her so. The
process of this information is given in detail by Teodorowicz.
"'Hundreds of times,' says Theresa Neumann, 'the Saviour
lets me know that I can suffer for others. I am not forced to
suffer. I could say I do not want to.' The manner in which
she receives the bids, so to say, for this pain is another proof

[191] Poray-Madeyski, p. 111.
[192] *ibid.*, p. 110.
[193] Teodorowicz, p. 375.
[194] *ibid.*, p. 375.
[195] *ibid.*, p. 374.

of her consciousness of it. There are two stages in this interior incitement to suffer for someone, but no other explanation of the details before she has consented to it. The second stage follows only after she has consented to this interior illumination and declared herself ready to suffer. The second stage is something entirely concrete, in which she receives an explanation of the circumstances, for whom she is to suffer, his name, where he lives, etc.; information that is necessary for her surroundings, that will be of assistance to her to concretely adapt herself to a certain thing or person." [196]

It is precisely these details given in her visions that cause apprehension. For it is doubtful whether this detailed information is necessary, since it cannot help the soul in question and would tend to diminish the perfection of the vicarious suffering; pride uses just such occasions to enter the unwary soul. It must also be remembered that suffering is not usually preceded by a consultation between Our Lord and His servants. For the heroic soul it is a gift of grace of the highest order, fuel for the flames of charity. Hence the desire for suffering is the expression of supernatural love both for Christ crucified and for His Mystical Body whose members it will benefit.

There is another trait in these " Suehneleiden " which seems strange. Nearly all these sufferings are alleged to take place on behalf of unknown individuals. Now, it is true that the saints have from time to time taken upon themselves expiatory sufferings; but hardly ever for persons unknown to them, and usually for some general purpose such as to avert persecution from the Church or to expiate the sins of a community. Also in the lives of the saints these expiatory sufferings were an exception, not the rule; in the life of Therese Neumann they follow each other with amazing rapidity and frequently last only a few hours. " As soon as one disease is disappearing, another one comes to replace it." [197] And Gerlich himself confesses that these illnesses " cannot be regarded as diseases in the ordinary sense." [198]

[196] *ibid.*, pp. 366ff.
[197] Poray-Madeyski, p. 112.
[198] Cited *ibid.*, p. 114.

Poray-Madeyski considers them to be manifestations of the hysteria that was never cured. The conviction that this assertion is more than merely probable is reinforced by the publicity given to the sufferings. Konnersreuth is full of the "Suehneleiden" of Therese, for which she is greatly admired, but which prevent her more often than not from attending Mass in the morning; though she frequently recovers sufficiently to receive Holy Communion privately in church by half-past ten a.m. One cannot help recalling St. Catherine of Siena in the last months of her life, who, almost dying, dragged herself to Mass every morning and stayed in church for hours despite her excruciating pains.

These criticisms are not meant to imply that Therese Neumann does not actually suffer, or that her sufferings could not be utilized by Almighty God for the good of souls. Whether sufferings are caused by an organic illness or by hysteria, the subject feels them all the same and, consequently, can offer them to God for the salvation of others. Yet there is a profound difference between a real organic disease which does not end after a comparatively short time and the temporary indispositions produced by hysteria—quite apart from the fact that it would need a very high degree of sanctity to remain spiritually unharmed by the publicity and general admiration accorded to such strange "Suehneleiden." The very fact that they prevent Therese from attending Mass and from accomplishing the duties of her state seems a further argument against their supernatural origin.

CHAPTER XII

Mystic States

ONE OF the distinctive phenomena in the spiritual life of Therese Neumann is her so-called mystic states. They are three in number: first comes the ecstasy or trance, during which she has her visions of the Passion and others; this is followed by a state of "childlike infatuation" in which her mental powers are those of a child of about four years of age or even less. In this state she "embraces all that she has seen in the great ecstasy and takes out of it what has made a special impression upon her, speaks about it and gives her opinion of it"; [199] but in a childish way, lacking completely the power of abstraction and generalization. A report by Fahsel, reproduced in Teodorowicz, gives a clear description of this state:

"She has almost entirely forgotten the memories of her natural former life and the attendant surrounding world. On awaking from the vision she often asks: 'Where am I?' In an agitated way (note the absence of calm ordinarily associated with mystic states, H.C.G.) she gropes around and asks: 'What is this?' If someone near her speaks, she asks meditatively: 'Who are you . . . ?' In this state, too, she cannot undertake any higher abstractions. Thus, she never mentions a mathematical number. When asked, 'How many Apostles were present there?' she does not say, 'Six,' but counts off: 'One there, one there, another there, and another there . . .' until she comes to six. Another psychic peculiarity is her childlike speech . . ." [200]

[199] Teodorowicz, p. 225.
[200] *ibid.*, p. 225.

Teodorowicz continues, giving his own experience: "There was no possibility of making clear to her what a bishop is or what the Holy Father is. Recourse would have to be taken to the simplest childish picture to make clear to her that the bishop is the great pastor . . . As with a little child, the simplest idea could be brought home to her only with difficulty, by circumlocution . . . It is said that in her childlike state she has not even the mentality of a four-year-old child. This is correct as regards her paucity of words in this condition. One can speak of a bishop or the Pope to a four-year-old child. There would be no necessity to adapt the idea as must be done with Theresa Neumann . . . And there is no consolation in the fact that she may have forgotten the number, 'four,' because when the pastor, during the description says, 'the four,' she answers, 'I do not know.'"[201] What follows this description is very suggestive, for it will offer a clue to this strange state.

"I had spoken to her a few days before," writes Teodorowicz, "and hence knew the timbre of her voice. *Now an entirely different person seemed to be speaking to me.* The spiritual substratum was as if that of another. The interior tone tempo had become faster. The sentences are given out in staccato fashion. The sound of the voice seems sharper and more highly pitched, while the 'du' (thou) that she uses toward all who are present is particularly noticeable. But at the same time the tone is one of a jolly, humorous person."[202]

The archbishop peremptorily repudiates the idea that this state could have anything to do with catalepsy and somnambulism, but he gives no conclusive proof against this thesis; and what he calls "the gifts of prophecy and wisdom, the workings of the Holy Ghost" which "reveal themselves"[203] in this state may, as we have seen in a former chapter, be called with equal justification telepathic powers intimately connected with catalepsy and somnambulism. But the most significant feature is the impression italicized by us, that "an

[201] *ibid.*, pp. 226f.
[202] *ibid.*, p. 227; my italics.
[203] *ibid.*, p. 231.

entirely different person seemed to be speaking to me." We have met this "entirely different person" before, and we shall meet her again presently when dealing with the "state of exalted rest." Teodorowicz, vindicating the supernatural character of the state of "childlike infatuation," writes: "The child-like characteristic is opposed to childishness and is founded in mysticism." [204] Now, it is quite true that genuine mystics are childlike, according to Our Lord's words: "Unless you become as little children . . ." But this refers to their childlike character, their purity and simplicity, not to some strange transitory state in which they cannot count up to three. And since the Archbishop writes that, whilst in that childlike state there seems to be quite a different personality in Therese, speaking with a different voice in a different tempo, the question arises: are we, perhaps, confronted here not with a mystic state, but with a condition of split personality?

On this subject Fr. Thurston makes some very pertinent remarks. After discussing the various "states" of consciousness of Mollie Fancher, the American Protestant visionary mentioned in ch. 8, he writes: "Again the whole question of Miss Fancher's five personalities seems to be a matter of considerable interest to the hagiographer. The normal Mollie, 'Sunbeam,' was absolutely sincere in disavowing all knowledge of anything which had been either said or done by 'Ida' or 'Pearl' (fancy names of her other personalities). It was the mere accident of her helpless condition, entailing more or less continuous observation, which led to the existence of the dissociated personalities being discovered at all. 'Pearl' might have eaten, or drunk, or stolen, or lied without 'Sunbeam' having the least idea that anything of the sort had happened. In the case of Therese Neumann we know that she who answers questions while the ecstasies of the Passion are in progress exhibits an intelligence of the most rudimentary kind, incapable even of counting numerals or of grappling with any abstract idea. Can we positively say that this is not a new personality—the more so that the history of the case with its spinal injuries, six years' immobility with paralyzed mem-

---

[204] *ibid.*, p. 233.

bers, supervening blindness, inability to absorb nourishment,[205] clairvoyant knowledge, and sudden recoveries of faculties in abeyance, exhibits striking analogies with the experiences of Mollie Fancher? " [206]

Notwithstanding Archbishop Teodorowicz, who mentions the case of Mollie Fancher only to dismiss it at once as entirely different from that of Therese,[207] we believe, with Thurston, that it offers a very interesting parallel. For is it not suggestive that there is present, observed by Teodorowicz himself, a difference in voice, pitch, rapidity of speech, etc., so great that he has the impression of an "entirely different person" speaking to him? This would point most strongly to a case of "split personality" resembling that of Mollie Fancher, who had five different personalities, making their appearance at different times.

Therese, too, has a third personality which appears in the "state of exalted rest." This follows generally on the childlike state, and is thus described by Teodorowicz:

"The tone of her ordinary manner of speech wherein the peculiarity of the soul and the inner being of a person are made known is tuned to another pitch. I was very much impressed by it. She speaks in a unique tone which she never uses otherwise. It is not even like that used in the childlike state. It is the tone of a thinker, a philosopher, and also a seer that lights up the future . . . All conclusions and expressions are given most competently . . . Even the tone of voice makes argumentation flee . . . The questions that are put to her and are not at times easy to answer, are immediately answered. The response comes even before the question is completely formed." [208]

". . . Another characteristic of this state," the Archbishop continues, "is the increase of the spiritual powers beyond the

---

[205] Fr. Thurston's footnote: " It seems a singularly suggestive fact that Therese Neumann, when in ecstasy, is able to receive an entire Host in Holy Communion without difficulty, but in her normal conscious state can only swallow a tiny particle."

[206] *The Month*, Jan., 1931, p. 29.

[207] Teodorowicz, p. 221.

[208] *ibid.*, p. 235f.

ordinary normal degree, as can be established from her speech, expressions, words . . . Theresa's flights move in the realm of philosophic thought." [209]

We have here, then, another personality, again with a different kind of voice and a different vocabulary, a personality that speaks even High German and not Therese's ordinary Palatinate dialect.[210] It is in this state particularly that she uses her telepathic powers in the service of others. So dissociated is this state from her normal personality that the voice that speaks can even say: "You cannot speak with Resl now, she is sleeping." [211]

This is a phenomenon not entirely unknown in the history of Christianity. For the same happened to the Montanist prophetesses we have mentioned before; this striking resemblance will be discussed further on. Teodorowicz, however, takes this to be a protection against pride, so that she may know nothing in her waking state about the powers she has whilst in trance. "By the exclusion of the extraordinary in her ordinary state," he writes, "she is studiously protected with a shield against too great temptations of self-exaltation." [212] He himself, however, proffers an obvious objection two pages later: "But may the information come to her from some other direction? Even if she does not in individual cases know what she has said while in the ecstatic state, still she knows from questions asked by letter or word that great trust is placed in her charismatic gifts . . . For self-complacency, to satisfy a desire, a little door could easily be opened even if the main door remains closed." [213] And he answers: "But her moral character lies open before us. There is reason enough to say for certain that she has escaped the enticing temptations of self-love and curiosity and has successfully overcome them and continues to fight against them." [214]

[209] *ibid.*, p. 238.
[210] *ibid.*, p. 236.
[211] Schimberg, p. 78.
[212] Teodorowicz, p. 421.
[213] *ibid.*, p. 424.
[214] *ibid.*

But if this is so, then why the whole elaborate apparatus in order to make Therese forget in her ordinary state what she has said in her trances? Does this not become quite superfluous? If one is truly humble, surely it is unimportant whether one is aware of extraordinary gifts because one remembers what was said in ecstasy, or because one is later told about it by others? And is it not the normal way in the life of sanctity that extraordinary gifts are bestowed upon a person only when she has reached a state in which they can no longer harm her humility? Of course, humility is never absolutely safe, but it would seem a somewhat defective providence that hides graces from souls lest they should become proud but forgets that these graces might be made known to them by others. We would submit that Archbishop Teodorowicz's enthusiasm has led him to explanations unsupported by the evidence he presents.

There remains the fact that these states, during which the ordinary personality of Therese is obviously in abeyance, have hardly a parallel in the lives of the canonized saints of the Church. In the opinion of Poray-Madeyski, however, a parallel can be found in the case-books of psychiatrists. "No less characteristic" (than other phenomena dealt with before), he writes, "appears . . . the sudden 'suspension' of this state of amyosthenic weakness and all its concomitant pains at the moment when Therese passes into the state of 'exalted rest,' which corresponds in everything to that particular (hysterical) state where takes place an apparently complete reconstitution of the personality, and where all the hysterical stigmata [215] . . . have disappeared or, rather, have been suspended, to reappear later when the subject returns to her preceding state. We would here mention once more, and at the same time emphasize, that this particular state, as well as the other similar psychic states, are all narrowly . . . attached to the hysteria, and enter all into its domain." [216] He concludes: "All these particular psychical states . . . demonstrate . . . that in the development of the neurosis there

[215] The word is here used as a medical technical term.
[216] Poray-Madeyski, p. 288.

has been progressively introduced the ever more active participation of the psychical sphere. Thus, the hysteria which had manifested itself in the beginning as a purely *functional* (*dynamique*) disease has revealed itself later as an authentic psycho-neurosis." [217] We see, then, that however striking the gifts displayed in this state of "elevated rest," a medical expert of the highest reputation considers them merely as phenomena in the hysterical ensemble.

Taking together the remarks of Fr. Thurston quoted at the beginning of this chapter, the opinion of Poray-Madeyski, and the subjective conditions of Therese during these states, considerable caution seems justified. Particularly instructive is the rapidity with which Therese frequently passes from one state into another, of which Teodorowicz gives a very striking example:

"On this day I experienced surprise after surprise. Just now Theresa is able to express herself synthetically and that far exceeding her ordinary state; now, suddenly, she loses all this accomplishment and uses the stammering expressions of a child. This is all very puzzling. Should the state of childlikeness, then, be the main constituent of the Passion ecstasy? But no. For the ecstasies terminate about a quarter to one and then the childlike state continues unbroken, without any regard for the religious ecstasies, for the rest of Friday. And today this state is interrupted for the second time by the state of exalted rest, and the childlike condition again returns. Can this striking change be explained physiologically or psychologically? Such changes, then, in which Theresa speaks as a child and then as a deep thinker, becomes childlike again and speaks in a manner strange to her; such changes defy every natural explanation." [218]

We have seen that there is a natural explanation, namely, that of split personality on a hysterical basis. If Mollie Fancher had five different personalities changing rapidly from one to another, the sudden changes between Therese's three, viz., her ordinary one, the one of the "childlike state" and

[217] *ibid.*, p. 289.
[218] Teodorowicz, p. 242.

that of the state of "exalted rest," would not necessarily call for the intervention of a supernatural agency. Cases of split personality are fortunately rare, but they do occur and must be taken into account when one is confronted with phenomena susceptible of this explanation.

From the point of view of the theologian, moreover, there are very grave reasons for not attributing these states of Therese to a supernatural agency. This is what Professor Waldmann wrote to me in a letter of January 6th, 1949. "The state of 'elevated rest,' in which from the unconscious Resl, deprived of her memory, speaks another personality, is not only 'unmystical,' 'without precedence in Catholic mysticism' as even Fahsel had to admit, and as has recently been sharply emphasized by Fr. Richstaetter, S.J. ('It occurs only in the case of hypnotized persons, hysterics of the gravest type, and spiritualist media'), but it is biblically, theologically and ecclesiastically equally unacceptable. In connection with the Montanist controversy (175–205 A.D.) it has been rejected by the universal Church after a discussion lasting thirty years. The Apologist Miltiades has written a treatise entitled *Peri tou me dein propheten en ekstasei lalein* (On its being unlawful for a prophet to speak in ecstasy), contested by Tertullian in a work containing six parts. Both writings are lost. But from the Church History of Eusebius and several allusions in Tertullian's other writings we are able to understand this principal question dividing the Church from Montanism. From the unconscious Montanus and his prophetesses there spoke the Holy Ghost or God the Father or Jesus Christ, giving their revelations which all aimed at a reform and greater severity of Church discipline."

In this connection it may be of interest to cite two passages from the Greek Church Father St. Epiphanius, upon which the present author came whilst investigating Greek Patristic teaching on the subject of ecstasy. Speaking of the prophet Ezechiel, Epiphanius says that he was "not as if carried away in an alienation of the mind," [219] contrasting him with Mon-

---

[219] ouch hos en ekstasei pheromenos, *Contra haereses* 48.3 (Berlin Corpus p. 224.7; Migne, PG 41.860C).

tanus who says: "Behold, the man is like a lyre and I as the plectrum. The man sleeps and I wake. Behold, it is the Lord who alienates the heart of a man and who gives a heart to men." [220] Epiphanius protests vigorously against such a conception of ecstasy. "The prophets," he writes, "were indeed in ecstasy, but not in an alienation of the mind (the word for both is the same in Greek). For Peter, too, was in ecstasy, not, however, in such a way as not to follow his reason, but as seeing other things, beyond what is ordinarily seen by men . . . St. Peter was not in an alienation of the mind. For when he heard the words, "Arise, kill and eat," he did not obey like one whose mind is enfeebled, but he says to the Lord: No, Lord, etc." [221]

St. Epiphanius, then, describes and condemns in the Montanist prophets exactly the same state as that in which Therese Neumann gives her teaching: it is a state of unconsciousness: "The man sleeps and I (whoever may be this mysterious other personality) am awake." It is the same dissociation in trance between the ordinary personality of the person and the trance personality, the one knowing nothing of what the other says or does. The Church Fathers, dealing with this phenomenon, did not regard it as a protection of the humility of the prophet but, on the contrary, as a sign of the spuriousness of his experiences. The true prophets and Apostles, as Ezechiel and St. Peter, retained all their powers of thought and will, that is their personality, even whilst most intimately united to God. We find the same in the lives of the later mystics; we need only recall St. Theresa who, in obedience to her directors, went so far as to show contempt to her visions of Our Lord; or St. Margaret Mary, who wished to refuse the

[220] idou, ho anthropos hosei lyra kago hosei plektron; ho anthropos koimatai kago gregoro. idou, kyrios estin ho existanon kardias anthropon kai didous kardian anthropois, ibid. 48.4 (Berlin p. 224.28ff., PG 861A).
[221] gegonasi de en ekstasei hoi prophetai, ouk en ekstasei logismon, gegone gar kai Petros en ekstasei, ouchi me parakolouthon to logo, alla horon anti tes kathemerines akolouthias hetera para ta tois anthropois horomena . . . ouk en en ekstasei phrenon ho hagios Petros. hote gar ekousen to " anastas thyson kai phage " ouch hos me ton noun erromenos epeisthe, alla phesi pros ton kyrion " medamos, kyrie," etc., ibid. 48.7 (Berlin, p. 228.14ff., PG 41.865A).

revelations she was told to communicate to others. They were never unconscious, with another personality speaking through them. It is true they were in ecstasy, with their limbs rigid and unable to move; but their superior powers were fully awake. The Lord might speak *to* them, but He did not speak *through* them as through an impersonal instrument.

Teodorowicz denies that this is so in the case of Therese Neumann; but this is insufficient to explain the phenomenon that when in the state of " exalted rest," some unknown voice speaking High German instead of her Bavarian dialect declares " Resl " to be asleep and makes statements far above her normal capacities. She herself says that in this state she feels " so close to the Saviour," [222] but this does not explain her suddenly speaking as quite a different person.

" It is equally important," writes Professor Waldmann, " that St. Thomas, *Secunda Secundae,* q. 173, a. 3, and referring to I Cor. 14:32, speaks about this disputed question between Montanists and Catholics and decides in the sense that the prophet, during imaginary visions and in the contemplation of the Divinity, can be alienated from his senses, but that after the ecstasy he must be able to state what he has seen. It must not happen as with Montanus and his Prophetesses, who ' *mente turbata sicut arreptitii, ut dixerunt Priscilla et Montanus.*' The famous commentators of the Angel of the Schools, Cajetan and Silvius, took over this traditional doctrine, and Benedict XIV takes from them the three important theses: ' Ecstasy is diabolic . . . if the person subject to it *loquatur mente turbata, quasi actus ab alio et quasi alius loquatur per eum; si post alienationem non recordetur eorum, quae dixit cum esset alienatus, et ea quae dixit, repetere nesciat.*[223] *Post Cajetanum bene adnotavit Silvius* (in IIa IIae, q.173, a.3) *eos, qui extasi corripiuntur, loquentes sub persona Christi vel*

[222] Teodorowicz, p. 243.

[223] If the person " speaks with a disturbed mind, as if acted upon by another, and as if another were speaking through him; if, after the alienation, he does not remember what he said whilst alienated, and cannot repeat the things he has said." Benedict XIV, *De Beatificatione,* c. 49, n. 6.

alienius Sancti, quasi actus ab illo, aut seduci aut seducere.' [224]
According to Silvius l.c. those cannot be recognized as true
prophets or mystics who, alienated from their senses while this
state lasts, speak of something as seen by them, but afterwards
do not know what they have seen and refer to what they have
said whilst alienated."

Professor Waldmann continues, " On this crucial point in the
question of Konnersreuth, Professor Mager, Salzburg, has put
his finger in the Salzburg *Katholische Kirchenzeitung,* 1932.
He warns most insistently not to believe in Konnersreuth and
the Konnersreuth movement. 'The Konnersreuth movement,'
he writes, 'is already on the road of error.' He demands an
immediate ecclesiastical investigation of the matter and concludes his article with the words: ' Unless it be made possible
that the ' state of elevated rest ' . . . be most carefully examined by a commission of very experienced experts, it would
be better Konnersreuth disappeared into oblivion . . .'

" The decision of the Universal Church against Montanism
and the matter of its ecstasies was of the most fundamental importance. Through it the Church has erected a wall of
division between mysticism and occultism of all sorts, between
true and false prophets, against spiritualism, shamanism and
sorcery. She will always stand by this decision. Trances
even to split personality, such as they are the presupposition
of all strange knowledge and faculties of the media, are in
contrast to natural, and more especially to supernatural,
ecstasy. States such as the state of ' childlike infatuation ' and
still more unequivocally the state of ' elevated rest ' remind one
of the phenomenon of ' possession,' whether diabolical or
psychological. In the case of Therese Neumann, the latter
supposition will probably still be sufficient. In the Middle
Ages she would probably have been exorcised. Even Fr.
Richstaetter was of this opinion, at least for some time. The
science of parapsychology causes us even here to reckon more
with natural factors."

[224] " After Cajetan, Silvius has well noted that those who, being carried
away by ecstasy, speak in the person of Christ or of another Saint, as if
acted upon by him, are either seduced or seducers." *ibid.*

The opinion of this learned theologian, who has made a special study of parapsychology and the distinctions between true and false mysticism, cannot be lightly disregarded. The observations on the many statements made by Therese in the state of "elevated rest" (see especially ch. IX) confirm the view of the professor. At the least, caution is necessary before it may be assumed that these states are supernatural, since they can be paralleled not by examples from the saints and the true mystics, but only from heretical prophetesses and spiritualist media.

CHAPTER XIII

Therese Neumann and Father Naber

I is with the greatest diffidence that we approach this chapter on the delicate relationship between a priest and his penitent; but the case of Therese Neumann is well-nigh inexplicable unless some account and interpretation be given of it. The accessible material for this chapter is very scanty, but still there is sufficient to make an examination possible.

When I first met Fr. Naber my impression was that of an excellent, devoted parish priest, amiable and courteous, obviously loved and venerated by his parishioners. I have had no occasion to change this opinion. It was God's incomprehensible wisdom that placed in his flock a person whose presence posed such unusual problems. Needed here was an authority on mystical theology and parapsychology, one acquainted by long experience with the most varied and difficult types of penitents. But Konnersreuth is a small Bavarian village, neither Carmelite monastery nor school of theology. Therefore, if this chapter suggests that certain changes of direction might have been more prudent, it is not with the intention of imputing blame to Fr. Naber nor of asserting ourselves as more competent (we have as advantages absence of personal relationship and another perspective): we would only indicate to the reader certain discrepancies that exist between this situation and the procedure recommended by the Doctors of the Church in similar circumstances. Human nature is not infallible despite the most faultless intentions; mistakes are always possible; and because of the peculiarity of circumstances in the present case, we think that they were almost inevitable.

Fr. Naber has been Therese Neumann's constant confessor and spiritual director from her thirteenth year. About five years after this association had begun there happened the accident at the fire, followed by its long series of illnesses. During these illnesses Fr. Naber " saw in her only an example of a good Christian submitting to the will of God . . . nothing beyond that." [225]   But when the strange cures began, his attitude changed; he begins to take a quite particular, and most uncritical, interest in her and all that happens to her. For example: of the first visions of Thérèse of the Child Jesus " the pastor . . . carefully remembered every word;" [226] he hastens to find a passage in the Little Flower's writings cited in one of these visions; [226] and when, after another miraculous cure, Therese's mother very sensibly objects that she ought not at once to exchange her warm bed for the cold night air in order to go to church, the priest takes Therese's part: " If St. Thérèse was there to help you, let's go at once! " [227]

Thus, even before the stigmatization begins, Fr. Naber is already quite convinced that the happenings at Konnersreuth are of a supernatural character. When the stigmata appear, no vestige of doubt seems to remain. When, according to Von Lama, " Therese's parents called Fr. Naber, he said to her: ' In obedience, let me see the wounds of your hands and feet.' What he saw moved him so vehemently that it required considerable time for him to regain his composure." [228]

This short account provides the key to all that will follow. Fr. Naber's very first words set the tone of the scene. " In obedience "—that means: this is a very solemn occasion, my whole authority as your confessor and director must be brought into play. This was not the most fortunate opening; for it showed Therese at once that what had happened to her was a very serious and important matter, to be treated with

---

[225] Teodorowicz, p. 161.
[226] *ibid.*, pp. 146 and 149.
[227] Poray-Madeyski, p. 54.
[228] Von Lama, p. 49.

utmost respect.[229] And when she had shown the wounds, " it required considerable time for him to regain his composure." It is important for priests—as it is for doctors—to control their emotions and remain calm and unperturbed even in the face of very unexpected events. Yet for Fr. Naber the sight cannot have been completely unexpected, since he had been informed before he came. It would have been more satisfactory, and his view of the case would command more confidence, had he shown himself unmoved and ready to examine the spectacle coldly and critically. Instead, he was so overcome that he cannot be regarded as an objective observer, for, without further investigation, " since those days he has devoted himself entirely to the responsible duties of this extraordinary phenomenon." [230]

Fr. Naber then, as we wrote in a preceding chapter, informed the local press of the events in his parish. As he told me himself, he did it because many rumors had been spread abroad and journalists had approached him with the request for authentic material. The normal procedure would

[229] Cf. St. John of the Cross, *Complete Works*, I, pp. 145ff. " There are some (directors) whose way and method with souls that experience these visions cause them to stray, or embarrass them with respect to their visions, or guide them not along the road of humility, but encourage them to fix their eyes upon them in some way (for which reason they remain without the true spirit of faith) and edify them not in faith, but lead them to speak highly of those things. By doing this they make them realize that they themselves set some value upon them, or make great account of them, and, consequently, their disciples do the same . . . such confessors, when they see their penitents are receiving visions from God, beg them to entreat God to reveal them to themselves also, or to say such and such things to them, with respect to themselves or to others, and the foolish souls do so, thinking that it is lawful to desire knowledge by this means . . . whereas, in truth, it is neither God's will nor His pleasure."

[230] Cf. Fr. Gabriel of St. Mary Magdalen, *Visions and Revelations in the Spiritual Life*, p. 11: " In many cases there is an exaggerated esteem for these heavenly favours, as they are considered to be, and this esteem is forthwith extended from the graces themselves to the persons who believe themselves so favoured. Undoubtedly they are saints! All the opinions of these souls, so enlightened by God, must be taken seriously! When a director becomes thus enthusiastic over his Philothea, the rôles are interchanged, and it is the visionary who becomes the director, whilst the priest submits himself as the docile disciple of his spiritual child."

have been to refuse to make a statement until the diocesan
authorities had been informed. This, however, was not done.
Fr. Naber was by now so convinced of the authenticity of the
phenomena and of the profit the Church would derive from
the publicity that he acceded to the wish of the journalists,
even going so far as to write the articles for the local newspaper himself.

In this connection the testimony of one who knows Fr.
Naber well may perhaps be of interest. This person said to
him in the year 1926, soon after Konnersreuth had begun to
be a "place of pilgrimage": "Father, if I had been parish
priest of Konnersreuth in your place, the affair of Therese
Neumann would not have been brought to the notice of the
public." Whereupon he replied: "No, this had to be done
ad majorem Dei gloriam." And the other: "*Vel ad scandalum
Ecclesiae.*"

This is, perhaps, the clue to the whole extraordinary story
and the amazing publicity it has received. I owe to Professor
Waldmann the following psychological explanation of Fr.
Naber's attitude:

"Fr. Naber was, and probably still is, so absolutely convinced of the divine and miraculous character of the events
concerning Therese Neumann that he would go through fire
for it. He had been especially impressed by the fact that
Therese was stigmatized in Passion Tide of 1926. Seeing that
he did not know, or appreciate, the enormous importance of
the medical diagnosis (sc. hysteria) of the year 1920, Therese's
cure of her blindness on the day of the Little St. Thérèse's
beatification, the cure of the paralysis on the day of her
canonization, as well as the complete restoration of her power
to walk on the day of her death and the sensational cure of
the appendicitis with visions of light and audition of voices,
might have convinced a more critically minded theologian
than Fr. Naber. The attitude of Professor Wutz and of the
convert from Calvinism, Gerlich, is proof of this. And after
all this, just as Fr. Naber *expected*, the stigmatization in
Passion Tide, the seal on the divine origin of the previous
events. From now on a further critical attitude would have

been lack of faith, as far as his ecclesiastical and theological conscience was concerned . . . However, the 'supernatural' development rose even higher. The highwater mark of the events of Konnersreuth is not so much the 'inedia,' as the almost simultaneous discovery of certain super-normal states: apart from the state of ecstasy also the state of 'infatuation' and of 'elevated rest,' with their astonishing supra-normal knowledge and abilities. Now the visitors who were admitted listened to a personality, speaking out of the unconscious Resl, who searched the hearts and possessed also knowledge of physical diseases . . . Hence, from that time, a completely blind belief in the supernatural in Therese and the attempts to explain everything in this sense." [231]

Therese having thus been launched, events took their natural course, and Fr. Naber became what Teodorowicz calls her "mediator." [232] The archbishop enumerates the various reproaches that are brought against Therese's director. "He can hardly satisfy everyone. By some he is accused of too much forbearance and leniency towards Theresa Neumann, while others find fault with him because he does not subject her to difficult tests. Again, others protest that he influences her by his questions, and others that he is trying to make a world oracle of Konnersreuth." [233] In fact, all these accusations, which Teodorowicz represents as if they were quite different, can be reduced to one: Fr. Naber is the driving power behind Therese Neumann. And from the objective account of the examining professor, reproduced in the chapter on *Publicity and Investigation,* it seems that there is certainly truth in this. A particularly disconcerting feature is that Fr. Naber constantly questions her during the trances, interprets every word and gesture,[234] discusses every detail, directs the visitors in and out of the room at the right moment and be-

---

[231] Professor Waldmann in a letter to me of Jan. 6th, 1949.

[232] Teodorowicz, p. 46.

[233] *ibid.*

[234] Cf. Gabriel, *op. cit.,* p. 54: " Often the director has to be content with inadequate replies, and he must also beware lest he himself suggest the replies in his questions. Such a proceeding would be simply an illusion."

comes fussed and excited if anyone attempts to make investigations not approved by Therese and her parents.

Teodorowicz, answering the objection that Fr. Naber did not subject her to difficult tests, writes: " He has given her various tests to find out whether the ego or the human will plays a part in her ecstasies and visions. His examinations and tests are entirely in accordance with critical scientific methods, so that the results of them would not in any way be below those that might be undertaken by a scientific commission." [235] The only examples of these " examinations and tests . . . entirely in accordance with critical scientific methods " which I have been able to find are the following: " Father Naber . . . wishes to make a test to find out if Theresa's imagination did not play a part in the ecstasy pictures.[236] He utilized the fact that her visions are generally in conformity with the ecclesiastical year. And on the Feast of St. Benedict, when Theresa had an ecstasty, he suggested with urgent entreaty that she should behold the beautiful picture of the departure of the saint from his sister, St. Scholastica. ' Ask the Saviour, Resl,' the pastor begged her, ' that you might see this scene.' He repeated these words several times. But all his efforts were in vain. Then he wanted to know if a vision which was in progress could be lengthened by her influence. Theresa had a holy joy in her ecstasy on one All Saints' Day, when she saw the heavens opened and all the saints in their glory. The vision was coming to an end as he entreated Theresa, saying: ' Resl, pray to the Saviour that you might be able to retain this vision a little longer.' She tried to obey his request but her efforts were in vain. She could not make the vision stay a second longer." [237]

There is a disarming, but nevertheless dangerous, naïveté about all this—both in the priest who made the experiment and the archbishop who regards it as a scientific test. For it will be obvious even to a not particularly critical observer that

[235] Teodorowicz, p. 47.
[236] Even in the admittedly supernatural " ecstasy pictures " of the saints the imagination generally plays a part, hence the possibility of error which is always present.
[237] Teodorowicz, p. 433f.

whatever Fr. Naber said to Therese, his strong expectation was that the visions would *not* be influenced by his words. Now, in a state of telepathic relationship it is the *mind* that influences another mind, not a verbal order given against the expectation and wish of the influencing mind. As we have seen, it has always been Fr. Naber's firm conviction that Therese's visions are supernatural; his dealings with her would be incomprehensible on any other supposition. Hence we do not think it unjust to say that his tests were made not with the ardent desire to learn the truth whatever it might be, but to prove that the phenomena are supernatural. Therefore any test in the manner of those described above, if undertaken by Fr. Naber, is of questionable value. There are other tests he might have made that would have influenced a critic more decisively in her favour: we mean tests of her humility. If he had opposed her visions; if he had ridiculed them—as has happened to most of the saints—and if she had humbly borne this opposition while the visions continued; then, indeed, their supernatural origin would have been more firmly established. Unfortunately we have been unable to find evidence of any such tests; hence one can accept the position of Teodorowicz only with the utmost reserve since, according to Dom Aloys Mager, his book " becomes, for the reader as well as for the author, though without their realizing it, an apology and not, as one would have liked, an exposé, a piece of research, the attempt of a scientific explanation of the facts. Thus, the author proposes as experts, enthusiasts of Konnersreuth who do not at all deserve an absolute confidence." [238]

Since, then, after the final " proof " of the supernaturalness of the case by the appearanc of the stigmata all further doubt would have been a violation of conscience, Fr. Naber had no alternative but to accept whatever Therese might say when in ecstasy, and his tests were made to confirm this view—a procedure not normally followed by prudent directors, even if they are convinced of the sanctity of their penitents. In connection with this, Teodorowicz writes: " I should like to add just a word about the pastor's obedience to Theresa Neumann.

[238] *Études Carmélitaines*, Oct., 1936, p. 154.

The only question here is one of obedience to the voices and apparitions manifested to Theresa, in so far as they give orders that are connected with her apostolate . . .[239] The pastor listens to Theresa's voices because he knows from experience that they do not err." [240] We have seen in preceding chapters that the inerrancy of Therese's voices is not so free from doubt as the Archbishop and her parish priest assume. But apart from this, as this whole complex of visions, revelations, voices and the rest is obviously very near to Therese's heart, it would be precisely here that her humility and obedience could best be tested by deliberately taking no notice of them from time to time. When the great St. Teresa was ordered by Our Lord in a vision to make a foundation in a certain place, her director forbade her to depart; and she humbly obeyed until events made it quite plain to him that the revelation was of divine origin.[241]

On the other hand, it is not only in the case of voices and visions that Fr. Naber submits to the wishes of his penitent. Père Bruno, O.C.D., reports the following incident during his visit to Konnersreuth:

"Fr. Naber says that the visions come suddenly, without concentration; that the love of the truth and the love of the Saviour are the characteristics of Therese. He authorizes me to give her Holy Communion tomorrow—if Therese wants it." Therese, however, did not want it, and the Carmelite continues: "I may accompany the Parish Priest. He will give her Holy Communion himself, for he must also communicate her mother who is ill and who would be surprised to see a stranger. I must look somewhat disappointed, for she says to the person who had introduced me: 'He can be quite satisfied with this, this is already much.'" [242]

---

[239] Cf. Tanquerey, *The Spiritual Life*, p. 710: "St. Theresa, who was favoured with so many revelations, did not want her directors to be guided in their decision solely by her visions. When Our Lord bade her found the reformed monastery of Avila, she humbly submitted her plan to her director, and when the latter hesitated, she consulted St. Peter of Alcantara, St. Francis Borgia, and St. Louis Bertrand."

[240] Teodorowicz, p. 83f.

[241] Cf. footnote 239 above.

[242] *Études Carm.*, pp. 165f.

This little scene throws considerable light on the relationship between director and penitent.   Fr. Naber is reluctant to give a direction, he leaves the decision entirely to Therese without taking account of the desires of his fellow priest.   Therese, on her part, does exactly what she wishes: she does not want to receive Holy Communion from this particular priest and makes the specious excuse that her mother (who must surely by this time have been accustomed to seeing strange priests about the house) might be surprised at receiving Holy Communion from a stranger.   But she does permit Père Bruno to be present when she receives, intimating that this is a privilege with which he ought to be satisfied.   It would not seem from this account that Fr. Naber is anxious to test either Therese's obedience or her readiness to relinquish her own desires; he lets this excellent opportunity slip by.

There is, however, another aspect of the relationship between Fr. Naber and Therese which is very pertinent to a discussion of the origin of the visions.   It is this, that in her states of "infatuation" and of "elevated rest," after the Passion trances, she is in telepathic communication with Fr. Naber.   This is quite innocent in itself—telepathy between persons who know each other well seems to be more frequent than is sometimes assumed; [243] and the intimacy of the spiritual relationship between confessor and penitent would be an extremely favourable background for the development of such phenomena. What is, however, dangerous is to assume supernatural revelation where there is nothing more than telepathic influence. This relationship may explain why Therese's visions of the feast of the day usually follow the Breviary account, even to reciting the antiphons in Latin.

This question of Fr. Naber's influence on Therese is discussed by Teodorowicz: " In the religious ecstasies there can be no question of any prompting by Fr. Naber.   He is entirely unacquainted with Aramaic, and his library contains no Ara-

---

[243] We refer the interested reader to the investigations made by Professor Rhine of Duke University into extra-sensory perception and kindred parapsychological experiences.   J. B. Rhine, *Extra-Sensory Perception*, London, 1935; *New Frontiers of the Mind*, London, 1938.

maic books." [244] This argument is rather remarkable in many ways. We have discussed the question of Therese's knowledge of Aramaic in a previous chapter. No one has ventured to suggest that it is due to Fr. Naber; it is believed that Professor Wutz has a good deal to do with it. On the other hand, Fr. Naber cannot be entirely without knowledge of it; for he is known to be a competent Hebrew scholar, and we have seen that he constantly repeats and translates the Aramaic words she is supposed to say for the benefit of the visitors. Moreover, this Aramaic amounts only to a few sentences; and the fact that Fr. Naber does not influence her here would not necessarily rule out his influence in other respects. The very fact that he continually explains and comments the visions of the Passion bespeaks a close relationship between director and visionary. So far is he from following the rule of the Mystical Doctor to take no notice of visions and such like phenomena that he eagerly questions her about every detail, suggesting what she might or might not have seen, wondering whether it was like this or like that. Poray-Madeyski gives an illuminating example of this which completely bears out the impressions of Professor Waldmann cited in an earlier chapter. This is the account as reproduced by Poray-Madeyski from the biography by Witt of Therese Neumann:

"After the visions of the martyrdom of St. Stephen, the following dialogue took place between Therese and the parish priest. Therese (as if awaking from a deep sleep): 'Where am I? What was that? I must try to remember . . .' Priest: 'Just think.' Therese: 'I know that young man so well . . . it's on the tip of my tongue.' Priest: 'It was St. Stephen.' Therese: 'And he who was sitting above, that's the same man, and in the same place, as when the Saviour was there.' Priest: 'That was the High Priest Caiaphas, etc.' After this explanation, Therese told the rest of her vision, and at the end the priest told her that St. Stephen had been a disciple of Jesus and that his martyrdom took place in the same year as the death of the Saviour. Then Therese took up the thread: 'Oh, he has known the Saviour! That's why he spoke in that man-

<hr />

[244] Teodorowicz, p. 47.

ner. Now I'm doubly pleased.' In a similar way Fr. Naber
helped Therese to understand the subject of the vision of the
martyrdom of St. Lawrence, which she did not succeed in
comprehending. She had seen a young man who was not the
Saviour, but his person and surroundings were totally unknown
to her. The Father, *with the help of the words of St. Lawrence related in the Breviary,* succeeded in making Therese
comprehend that it was this martyr of whom her vision
treated." [245]

Is a sceptical attitude under these conditions entirely without
warrant? We think not. And does it not seem at least probable that these visions might have been produced in the same
way as Professor Waldmann believes her first visions of the
Transfiguration to have been produced, namely, by telepathic
influence? Fr. Naber expects a vision of St. Lawrence on the
feast of the saint, and naturally he expects it to follow the
Breviary account (generally held to be legendary). This
vision takes place—but without Therese understanding what it
represented, that is without an illumination from the Holy
Ghost. Now, an expectant attitude on the part of the director
is precisely the one most favourable to the production of telepathic phenomena: eager expectation from the director, hence
increased receptivity on the part of the penitent, to say nothing
of the disastrous effect such procedure might have on the
natural vanity of the one thus made the centre of interest.

Nor is Teodorowicz's statement acceptable that "in the circumstances of the childlike condition that follows the great
ecstasies no influence on Fr. Naber's part can be adduced, for
the simple reason that Theresa Neumann does not brook any
persuasion or dictation. On many occasions I observed the
pastor's rôle under these circumstances. He is very calm and
treats Theresa like a child with whom he jests. His duty
narrows itself principally to mediation between visitors and
stigmatist." [246]   Here Archbishop Teodorowicz's refutation
misses the point. There is no question of Fr. Naber "per-
suading" or "dictating" to her in this state. This is impos-

---

[245] Poray-Madeyski, p. 86; my italics.
[246] Teodorowicz, p. 47f.

sible, for it is a trance state in which the normal consciousness is eliminated—and only persons in possession of their normal powers of reason and will can be persuaded or dictated to. The influence of Fr. Naber on Therese Neumann in this state is exercised through a subconscious relationship. If there were no such relationship it is difficult to see how he could act as "mediator" between Therese and her visitors. In fact, it is one of the remarkable traits of Konnersreuth that Fr. Naber is constantly in attendance on his penitent, always ready to explain, whether it be her visions or the advice she gives to enquirers. We are aware of no instance in the lives of the mystics where a director has assumed such a rôle; the saints were usually quite capable of communicating directly what they wished others to know.

This same holds good for the state of "elevated rest." Teodorowicz asserts that "in the state of elevated rest all influence of the pastor is out of the question." [247] The archbishop gives no proof for this assertion, so it is impossible to determine what his reasons might be. Evidently it is possible to be of a different opinion, for we have an account of Professor Waldmann, who writes: "The almost constant telepathic relationship with Fr. Naber, apart from his ordinary influence on her thought and will in his pastoral capacity and in that of having been her constant confessor from her thirteenth year, can hardly be over-estimated in their effect on these visions. *This is even more the case in the state of elevated rest.*"

That there exists a strong telepathic relationship between Therese and Fr. Naber seems to admit of little doubt, and is convincingly illustrated in incidents told by Teodorowicz himself. He writes: "Father Naber told me of another instance. He had business to attend to in Berlin. After his return Theresa told him that she had assisted at his Mass in Berlin. Then she described the church; a priest had served . . . In like manner Theresa also, when she was once staying in Waldsassen, assisted at a Mass that was celebrated by Father Naber in Konnersreuth. She heard the sermon . . ." [248] Teodorowicz

[247] *ibid.*, p. 48.
[248] *ibid.*, p. 413.

admits that these examples "have their analogy in the hidden forces of the natural sphere." [249]   What is of interest in our context is that it is strongly suggested by such instances that *there does exist a strong telepathic relationship between Fr. Naber and Therese Neumann.*   We do not claim that this is the only possible explanation or the most complete one of the events we are examining.   As we stated in the introduction, our purpose is not to give a decision (only the Church is competent to do this) but merely to place relevant material before the reader, much of which has been hitherto unavailable in English-speaking countries, so that certain aspects of this problem might be illuminated for him, perhaps for the first time.

Early in this chapter we mentioned certain discrepancies between the conduct of Fr. Naber and that suggested by the Doctors of the Church.   A few of these have already been indicated.   We would now, in conclusion, take several concrete examples in which the behaviour of ecclesiastical authorities, spiritual superiors and directors will be severely in contrast with that of the parish priest of Konnersreuth.   These are not selected arbitrarily, they are completely representative and can be paralleled by dozens of other similar situations throughout the history of the Church.

When Margaret Mary Alacoque first began receiving her visions she was treated with the utmost contempt by her companion religious; her illnesses were mocked and she was regarded as a *malade imaginaire*.   Our Lord was appearing to her with greater frequency, but each time she was violently opposed.   He gave instructions about her conduct at prayer, etc., which her Mother Superior absolutely forbade her to carry out; when theologians were consulted they accused her of having "illusions" and condemned her attraction for prayer. Finally, she was commanded by Our Lord to tell her community that she was to be a victim of expiation for their sins. This was too much for the good sisters; they said she was possessed by the devil, shunned her and when she passed them threw holy water on her as a gesture of their fear and horror.

[249] *ibid.*, p. 412.

On December 9th, 1531, Our Lady appeared to the un-educated Indian peasant, Juan Diego, who was still only re-ceiving catechetical instructions. She wanted a church built where she could love and be loved by the Indians. Juan went with his story to Bishop Zumárraga, who laughed him to scorn and sent him away. Four times Our Lady appeared to Juan and he begged her for a sign so that his vision might be be-lieved. Still the authorities mocked him; well-educated mem-bers of the conquering people, they refused to accept this apparition to a member of a supposedly inferior race. On the fourth appearance Our Lady bade him fetch some roses from the mountains and bring them to the Bishop. He folded the roses into his serape, took them to the bishop, and when he opened the serape, on it was stamped the image of the Virgin, a dark-skinned Lady bending her head with gentle courtesy and grace to her native children.

These are only two examples; many others would serve as well: Bernadette of Lourdes, whose parish priest used to say that if Our Lady had appeared to any other of the local chil-dren he could understand, but never to this stupid little girl; St. Teresa opposed in her reform of Carmel by confessors and authorities at every turn; St. John of the Cross imprisoned at Toledo for the same reason. The examples of the saints are without number, and each one follows in the steps of his Lord—His elect taking upon themselves their cross, being tried in the fire of opposition. The departure from this pattern would itself be sufficient reason for the greatest circumspection in one's approach to any seemingly supernatural experiences.

CHAPTER XIV

The Interior Life

As a kind of preface to the following two chapters I should like to cite passages from Fr. Thurston's series of articles in *The Month* on stigmatization. The reason for this will be made clear presently. He writes:

" There are . . . three antecedent considerations which strongly suggest that we should look for a pathological rather than a supernatural solution to the problem. The first . . . from a medical point of view . . . a bad family history. In the next place . . . before the development of the phenomena the subject has nearly always given evidence of a congenital predisposition to such disorders as tuberculosis or hysteria, or else has been exposed to some abnormal shock to the system, some terrible calamity or frightening episode which has brought on a severe attack of illness. Thirdly, that . . . the power which stigmatics not uncommonly exhibit are . . . associated with symptoms which the alienist physician would diagnose as probably indicative of some deep-seated neurosis. I refer particularly to the blindness, the deafness, the loss of speech . . . the aversion to food or drink . . . and the suddenness with which critical illnesses develop, only to be healed as suddenly by apparently miraculous cures." [250] A few paragraphs later he continues:

". . . I am inclined to think that . . . God for his own ends blessed and used faculties that were akin to those we must recognize in . . . Mollie Fancher . . . faculties which were preternormal rather than supernatural . . . It seems permissible to believe that such faculties in the stigmatisées men-

[250] *The Month,* March, 1931, pp. 240ff.

tioned (Gemma Galgani—who had not yet been canonized at
the time of this article's publication—and Marie de Jésus
Crucifié) may well have been associated with heroic sanctity,
but I would submit that similar phenomena need not necessarily be associated with heroic sanctity and that they belong
rather to a peculiar pathological condition . . . We might
quite reasonably expect to find genuine stigmatic phenomena
. . . in people who . . . were by no means saints, and were
inclined to exploit such manifestations for their own glorifica-
tion." [251]

I quote Fr. Thurston at length in order to indicate a problem; it is this: if sanctity is not necessarily proved by the
appearance of unusual manifestations; if such manifestations
are not, in themselves, a guarantee of their validity; in other
words, if we may not conclude from their presence and other
accompanying experiences to the presence of a ground of holiness from which they spring—then how can any progress be
made in our examination? As Fr. Thurston shows, and as we
have explicitly stated earlier, ultimately it is sanctity which
counts; the Church canonizes sanctity in the soul that shows a
close and constant union with God; the Church raises to the
honour of her altars those whose whole life is penetrated by
the one consuming desire to serve Him, to glorify Him, to
present to Him a life spotless and pure, a soul worthy of the
divine nuptials. Thus, if holiness is proof of the supernatural
origin of such phenomena as we have been discussing, then
holiness is what we must investigate.

Perhaps this suggestion may be resented by some, and I
admit that it would be very arrogant to pronounce upon the
holiness of a soul in accordance with some preconceived ideas.
This is an act of judgment only almighty God may make; only
He can see the agonies and indecisions, the difficulties and
temptations, in the suffering hearts of His children. His justice
is never without His mercy, unaccompanied: it is this that
gives man his hope. I do not presume, then, to judge; I only
hope to present to the reader whatever to me seems incom-

[251] *ibid.*, pp. 242ff.

patible with a high state of sanctity, begging him always to remember that these are *my* impressions, that they are not final, that God's ways are, in the last resort, unknown and hidden from our eyes. If I offend, if I seem to accuse, it is not intentional; and the responsibility for my words is mine. But I think the matter important enough to embark upon a discussion despite its being subject to possibilities of error and impertinence. But there is no other manner of summarizing with any degree of comprehensiveness the multiple aspects of our investigation.

Needless to say, the material available on the spiritual life of Therese Neumann is scant. Hardly any of the popular biographies touch on this, since it is in most cases beyond the scope and interest of their writers. It is to Archbishop Teodorowicz that we must turn for information; he alone would seem to have been aware of the necessity of a spiritual foundation to make fully intelligible the presence of *gratiae gratis datae*. The fact that he is our only competent source will explain not only his seeming omnipresence in the following pages, but also the fact that our criticisms appear most often to be directed at him. It is not his observation that is in question but his conclusions, which we feel are often naive and unwarranted in the light of a broader view of the circumstances and evidence. Finally, before proceeding, we would point out that enthusiasm is always dangerous, that it is inconsistent with the caution and suspicion which Holy Mother Church advocates and of which she sets us an example in her approach to her children. The Church has eternity on her side and we can aid her only by conforming to her will.

The fundamental virtue of the spiritual life, that on which the whole supernatural edifice must be raised if it is not to be a "house built on sand," is, as all the saints and textbooks of mystical theology tell us, the virtue of humility.[252] It is this, therefore, that must be examined first.

---

[252] Cf. Tanquerey, *op cit.*, p. 538. "And so, it can be said that without humility there is no solid and lasting virtue, and that on the other hand, through humility, all virtues grow and take deeper root in the soul. We may well conclude with the words of St. Augustine: 'Dost thou wish to rise? Begin by descending. You plan a tower that shall pierce the clouds? Lay first the foundations on humility.'"

There are, of course, degrees of humility. No Christian life can be wholly without it; but the higher and more extraordinary the graces, the greater the apostolic desires of the person, so much more profound must be the humility. The higher the stage a soul has reached on her way to perfection, the more subtle and powerful are the temptations to pride. For a soul attracting tens of thousands of visitors, who is constantly required to give advice on spiritual matters ordinarily far superior to her natural capacities, humility would be necessary to a degree little short of the heroic. Teodorowicz writes: " The question whether Theresa Neumann possesses this virtue is certainly the fundamental question of her interior life; all supernatural graces depend upon humility. Mystic graces without humility are always suspect as far as their source is concerned." [253] He goes on to say: " In this examination of humility it will make no difference whether or not feelings of self-love show themselves, because human weakness always accompanies such feelings. What is far more important is that the very foundation of her soul is to be dealt with." [254] This modification of the archbishop is not without its difficulties. That feelings of self-love show themselves *is* important; it is precisely their *appearance* that is in question, not their presence. If any person approaches sanctity there will obviously be motions of self-love (the soul is never so safe in this life as to be entirely free of them) but they will be so subtle and hidden that they will be noticed only by the soul herself and her confessor; in fact, the experience of the saints has been that these motions were mostly so faint that their confessors were unable to see them even when they were mentioned in confession. It is the very obviousness of these movements of self-love that militates against the presence of a high degree of humility.

The next assertion of the archbishop is no less ambiguous. He writes: " If, then, we wish to examine whether Theresa possesses this inner consciousness of her own nothingness and the power of divine grace, we must not . . . separate humility

[253] Teodorowicz, p. 28f.
[254] *ibid.*, p. 29.

from love. A soul favoured with so many extraordinary graces
would assuredly fall a victim of its own self-love if it dispensed
with the all-powerful source, the mystic love of Christ . . .
For this reason I first undertook to examine the mystic relation
of Theresa Neumann to Christ and then to proceed to an examination of her humility. My guiding principle will be, then,
since Theresa Neumann is warmed through with the mystic
love of Christ, we can confidently examine her humility." [255]

It is doubtless true that humility cannot be separated from
love; love is the end of all the virtues; but the soul's mystical
relation with Christ is a secret thing which can only be shown
forth in the life and actions of a virtuous soul by her external
conduct. We must, therefore, proceed from the visible to the
invisible. Teodorowicz is here guilty of the *petitio principii*.
Rather than testing the graces by humility, he proves the
humility by the graces. This is a serious error in logic and
demonstrates nothing. Not in this way shall we make progress,
but by referring directly to Therese herself as she appears to us
in the Archbishop's book *sine* commentaries and conclusions as
much as is possible.

"We are in possession of a saying of Theresa's which gives
us an insight into the source of her humility. She once said:
'Humility comes from love.' This is one of those deep and
simple expressions that always brings up the question: Whence
did this simple child of nature get so much light in the things
of the spirit? The great teacher of the Church, St. Francis de
Sales, whose works Theresa had never read, describes the
character of humility thus: 'Not from humility to love, but I
go from love to humility.'" [256]

The Archbishop represents Therese as more illiterate than
she really is. Our information is that she had read the *Introduction to the Devout Life;* [257] but even if she were not directly
familiar with the writings of the saint there are other sources.
Fr. Naber is a great admirer of St. Francis de Sales and, according to a letter from Professor Waldmann (who was a

[255] *ibid.*, p. 31.
[256] *ibid.*, p. 32.
[257] Poray-Madeyski, p. 4.

fellow student of Fr. Naber in the seminary), he directs Therese in the spirit of St. Francis de Sales. It is not *necessary*, then, to posit a supernatural illumination in order to account for "those deep and simple expressions."

We are then given a distinction between "the humility that hides the grace of God under a bushel" and "the humility that finds its authorization in the Saviour's words: So let your light shine before men." [258] This is not a principle which can be applied univocally, i.e., identically in all circumstances; for the possibility of scandal to others and danger to oneself must always be taken into account. Circumspection and a thorough knowledge of the situation are necessary before a decision can be given. Besides, we have the witness of the saints who, all too aware of the frailty of human nature, constantly strove to hide any unusual graces they received. They were distressed if others surprised them in ecstasy (we remember St. John of the Cross gripping the grille in a Carmelite parlour to prevent himself from being raised in the air) and if they could not hide them because God desired to proclaim them their behaviour made it clear to all that they suffered from the unwelcome publicity.[259]

In order to make our meaning clearer we should like to present here two similar accounts; one of St. Catherine of Siena, the other of Therese Neumann. This will be instructive because the situations are remarkably alike, if not in detail at least in substance. Both women were slandered in their virginal honour, both were blamed for their inability to take food. Here, from Alice Curtayne's fine biography, is St. Catherine: "Catherine took charge of a leprous woman . . . whom everyone had abandoned because her wicked tongue was almost more insupportable than . . . her disease . . . By way of recognition, Tecca (the old woman) slandered Catherine's honour in a most vile fashion . . . The old

---

[258] Teodorowicz, p. 32.

[259] Upon receiving the stigmata, St. Gemma Galgani's immediate preoccupation was—how to conceal this occurrence whilst still making her customary visits to church in the morning for Mass and in the evening for prayer. *Vide* Philip Cochlan, C. P., *St. Gemma Galgani*, p. 72.

woman's incredible malice afflicted her profoundly, but she said nothing and continued to nurse her lovingly . . . She was consoled when Tecca died repentant." [260] "To avoid singularity she, too, would partake of a morsel . . . But the moment any food entered her stomach her face swelled and grew disfigured . . . Alessa besought her not to eat since it cost her so much, but Catherine's invariable reply was that she wished she could eat so as not to look so odd." [261] Now Therese:

"Tender and deeply wrought is the feeling of justice that she demands for herself . . . Thus, she sued a newspaper reporter who calumniated her and touched upon her virginal honour. She becomes sensitive, too, if her convictions happen to be wrong from an ecclesiastical viewpoint. She complained about certain reproaches that were made to her: 'Is it my fault if I do not eat anything, or if I have the marks of the wounds? I am not responsible for that. What do they want of me, anyway?'" [262] Self-denial and loving submission are the principal constituents of humility; without these it can only be a pale shadow of its true self. And it was Our Lord who said, "Deny thyself and take up thy cross."

Our present inquiry is complicated by the fact that there are no unquestionable examples in Teodorowicz's book or, for that matter, in any other account known to me that might serve here as a guide. Therefore, inadequate though it may be, we must restrict ourselves to the material at hand and attempt to illustrate our thesis with what we have. We select representative incidents from Teodorowicz.

"Father Fahsel tells us: 'One evening, in company with a learned Dominican priest, I visited her. We spoke about the difficult question of faith and grace. I brought forward something said by St. Thomas and she replied: "Why do you say it in such a complicated way, Father?" As I began to explain

[260] A. Curtayne, *St. Catherine of Siena*, p. 32f. It is interesting to note that Margaret of Cortona also endured this particularly severe mortification.

[261] *ibid.*, p. 57.

[262] Teodorowicz, p. 39.

the statement of the Angelic Doctor she at once took part and answered in so wonderful and deep a manner that tears of emotion began to well in the eyes of the Dominican." ' [263] I should like first to point out the unsatisfactory and incomplete manner of recounting that characterizes most of these stories. In the present one we are not told what question of faith and grace was discussed (St. Augustine has written volumes on these problems); we are not told St. Thomas's comment, nor are we given Therese's answer, so we cannot determine its profundity or appositeness. Under these conditions it is almost impossible to appraise adequately the event. However, this much is clear:

(*a*) In his enthusiasm Archbishop Teodorowicz neglects to consider that if St. Thomas (who is the Common Doctor of the Church and who says that he wrote for beginning students) dealt with this in a complex fashion, it was probably because the subject demanded it; and that two priests, one of them a member of the religious order whose specific duty in the Church is to preserve the Thomist tradition, were interrupted in a theological discussion without any solicitations from them.

(*b*) There are certainly many precedents in history of wisdom being given to the unlearned. We know that St. Catherine of Siena, unlettered though she was, received the deepest theological wisdom as an infused gift of the Holy Spirit; but it is not the knowledge itself that is here in question (knowledge does not constitute sancity), it is the *manner* in which it is displayed and the *purpose* to which it is put. It is presumption, or the absence of it, which must be determined.

Another example: " On one occasion, as a gentleman who was a witness to her ecstasy left the room, I heard her cry out: ' Foolish fellow, he asked himself in his soul if there is a Saviour, because everything is going so badly in Germany now. He asks if there is a Saviour, and I would be ready a thousand times to offer my life for Him.' " [264] The comparison of a soul in doubt at the appalling conditions in his country

[263] *ibid.*, p. 167.
[264] *ibid.*, p. 24.

and Therese's readiness for martyrdom seems unnecessarily invidious and accusing. Is not in such circumstances the first duty of the lover of God to reassure, to console, to instil into the wavering soul an increase of love and confidence?

Again from Father Fahsel, an admirer of Therese Neumann, comes another story: " She says to a priest who reads his Breviary in her presence: You cause the Saviour a severe trial by reading Latin to Him for an hour. But tell Him simply: My God, I love you." [265]   Limitations of space forbid a thorough analysis of the error in this over-simple pronouncement on the manner in which God is most suitably glorified; it is sufficient to point out that the Divine Office is the official prayer of the Church and, with the exception of the Sacrifice of the Mass, is the most perfect praise that can be offered to Almighty God. Another time Therese had occasion to say: " Do not read to the Saviour so much of what is in books. He knows very well what is in them. It is with the heart that one must speak to Him . . ." [266]   This is no doubt true, but we are hardly *telling* Our Lord the contents of our spiritual reading; rather, on the advice of the saints and great spiritual directors, we devote certain periods to such reading in order to learn better what God is and what He wants of us. In truth, the remark that the Saviour knows what is in books, like most eager simplifications, says too much. He knows equally well what is in our hearts, and if we were to press this to its logical conclusion we would have to say that we ought not to speak to Him at all. This may seem a trifle harsh, but we have here one of the fundamental errors of the Quietists, anathematized by the Church. It may be said that Therese is an unlettered peasant girl, that her utterances may perhaps be explained in terms of some kind of intellectual inferiority complex. But this is not at all the point we are trying to make. There is no instrument God cannot use for his glory; and we honour today as saints some whose intellectual gifts were anything but promising (remember the Curé d'Ars who had difficulties in mastering his theology). Here it would

[265] Poray-Madeyski, p. 96.
[266] *ibid.*, p. 96.

not seem that any particular glory was given to God; for the statements quoted are in direct contradiction to the instructions of the Church, which speaks with the voice of the Holy Spirit.

We have seen in other contexts, when discussing the prominent position her own person occupies in the visions and when dealing with the prediction of her various states in trance, that there exists a pre-occupation with herself not ordinarily found in such circumstances. The same feature is evident in Therese's attitude to what she regards as her mission. We cited earlier the revealing passage from Teodorowicz—" Where she is convinced that there is no honest attitude to the Konnersreuth events, she becomes stern and hard, inexorably hard." [267] The Archbishop gives the reason for this attitude a few pages before: " We will now gaze upon the soul of Theresa Neumann and inquire about her humility . . . . It was foretold her by the voice in the vision, namely, that these penetrating graces are given her for the good of souls in her universal apostolate; therefore she cannot admit that the instrument of divine Providence fails to recognize these graces.[268] And hence, she cannot indifferently regard how obstacles malevolently pile up, having for a purpose the eradicating of these extraordinary graces. Theresa possesses, as is patent from her many protestations, a conviction of her own unworthiness, a conviction that is joined with lack of confidence in herself. She possesses great confidence in and great trust in the graces working in her soul." [269]

Again we meet an impoverishment of detail. Teodorowicz is unfair to his subject; he lists only protestations to illustrate her distrust in herself when one would prefer actual examples; whereas trust in her graces, as preceding chapters have shown, is evidenced by innumerable facts. But the Archbishop's

[267] Teodorowicz, p. 40.

[268] Cf. Gabriel, *op. cit.*, p. 91: " All exaggerated esteem for visions must be banished. It is even preferable that we should prefer not to meet with such phenomena in our spiritual life, and should be loth to believe in their authenticity. No attitude is safer than this! "

[269] Teodorowicz, p. 36.

apology for her attitude in the face of opposition to her graces
demands closer examination, for it disregards a very important
point and is therefore misleading. It has been the invariable
attitude of the saints to regard opposition to their mission,
whatever it might be, as the seal of its authenticity; however
much their human susceptibilities might smart under it, their
supernatural faith welcomed it as the mark of the divine
approval because they saw in it the sign of the Cross and knew
that God permits His lovers to be tried in this fashion. They
also knew that this opposition would, in the end, fulfil God's
plans far more effectively to His greater glory than their own
wishes. For God is the author not only of the graces but also
of the trials of His saints, according to the words of St. Paul
that to those who love God all things work together for their
good. And if the opposition should even destroy their life
work—this, too, would be the operation of Divine Providence.
For theirs is a life of faith. When St. Ignatius of Loyola was
asked how long it would take him to resign himself to the de-
struction of the Society of Jesus, he replied: about a quarter
of an hour. But Therese Neumann " cannot indifferently
regard how obstacles malevolently pile up " to prevent people
from believing in her. Perfect trust even when there seems no
ray of light in the darkness is a surer sign of love than trust in
any number of extraordinary graces.

Archbishop Teodorowicz is convinced of Therese's humility
because he is certain that " Theresa Neumann is warmed
through with the mystic love of Christ;" [270] by which he apparently means (the Archbishop's terminology throughout is
not of the clearest) a high degree of charity such as is required
for the mystic life of the soul. Now, it is quite true that profound love of Christ is impossible without profound humility;
for He has told us Himself that if we love Him we must keep
His commandments,[271] and one of these is to learn from Him
because He is meek and humble of heart.[272]

The " dynamic force in Theresa," writes Teodorowicz, " is

[270] *ibid.,* p. 31.
[271] John 14:15.
[272] Matt. 11:29.

the love of God that manifests itself in her love of the dear
Saviour.[273] "Theresa," he continues, "is as familiar with the
Saviour as a child. The confidential chats that she holds with
the Saviour, when she thinks she is alone in her room, breathe
such a natural childlike spirit that one could almost smile at
this confidential tenderness of spirit. Sometimes she acts
toward the Saviour like a spoiled child. She does not even
shrink from making little childish complaints to Him."[274] And
he goes on to write: "But tender, trusting, childlike and long-
ing love is strong love. Theresa is always ready to give her life
a thousand times for the Saviour."[275] Then follows the story
just quoted of her rebuke to the man who doubted that there
was a Saviour. Another instance cited by the Archbishop is
her remark to Gerlich: "Even when I speak to you I am thinking of the Saviour,"[276] a remark which may instructively be
considered in connection with the words of Our Lord (cited
by Teodorowicz in a different context), "Not everyone that
saith to me, Lord, Lord, shall enter into the kingdom of heaven,
but he that doth the will of my Father."[277] Teodorowicz says,
indeed, that "her will is directed entirely upon one thing, the
fulfilment of the divine will,"[278] but once more there is given
no conclusive proof of this; for the one adduced bears upon
resigning herself to her stigmatization, which had made impossible her original desire to become a missionary sister. But
if Poray-Madeyski's hypothesis of her as an hysterical case be
even probable, then this argument is insufficient because one
characteristic of hysteria is a general indifference of the
patient to his state of health. One raindrop does not make a
shower. Also, once this act of resignation has been made, she
received ample compensation in the veneration of vast multi-
tudes of people. Therese is reported as saying: "That is all
valueless; some praise me, others call me a deceiver. But that
does not make any difference to me; all that does not bring me

[273] Teodorowicz, p. 22.
[274] *ibid.*, p. 23.
[275] *ibid.*, p. 24.
[276] *ibid.*, p. 25.
[277] Matt. 7:21.
[278] Teodorowicz, p. 19.

closer to God." [279]   This is truly admirable, but does it not
flatly contradict the facts reported earlier in this chapter of her
being "inexorably hard" on those whose attitude to Konnersreuth she does not consider honest?   It is splendid to express
such sentiments in words, it is a good beginning; but they must
also be expressed in one's life if we are to believe in their
reality.

But may not all this be petty quibbling?   Does not Therese
show in the way she lives the Passion that she is really ani-
mated by an ardent love of Our Lord?   We have noticed in a
preceding chapter that her love of Our Lord as manifested
during the trances has sentimental qualities; and sayings like,
" I have no time for you now, Saviour, to talk to you; I must
sleep properly," seem hard to reconcile with that " mystic love "
admired by Teodorowicz.   It would, however, be unfair to
conclude from an isolated example; hence, we give a few more
instances that seem to justify doubt—instances that even Teodorowicz had some difficulty in reconciling with his favourable
opinion of Therese.   We have already cited her prediction of
trances and trance happenings immediately after Holy Communion, and the explanation the Archbishop gives of a " mystic
secretariate."   But it is nevertheless hard to understand that in
a soul perfectly absorbed in love of her Eucharistic Saviour the
few minutes whilst He is truly present within her should be
taken up with such predictions, whose only effect is to attract
attention to herself.   It is possible that such a thing could
happen, but during these moments of union the loving soul
usually withdraws from all other pre-occupations in order to
commune silently with her God.   There is, however, an even
more extraordinary occurrence:

" Anybody who has witnessed Theresa's deep excruciating
pain during her ecstasy can hardly understand how fire stirred
up in her soul can seem to be suddenly extinguished.   During
a pause that ended a series of scenes from the Passion of Christ
just before the crucifixion, Theresa was asked by the pastor
what she saw.   And she, who but a few moments before was

[279] *ibid.,* p. 21.

almost overcome with the pain of soul, speaks of her experiences in a manner that is astonishing to beholders. No glowing spark seems any longer to warm her words. Her speech, which during the ecstatic condition expressed pain, now that it is over, is calm, almost cold, without any enthusiasm . . . When asked she synthesizes what she saw and recounts: The Saviour was scourged, then a crown of thorns was placed upon His brow, then He appeared to the women, etc., and at the same time she adds the words that she heard. I am still under the impression of that antithesis. First the pain that she suffered with the agony of Christ . . . I am entirely overcome by the violence of the expression of pain and then the almost frigid answers that she gives to the pastor when he asks her: 'Resl, what happened to the Saviour?' 'He died,' she answers in an ordinary tone of voice as if it were something indifferent." [280] Then he continues: "One would expect that the necessary attendant circumstances of the Passion Scenes, such as the glowing love and sympathy, would continue to express themselves . . . . But here we are disappointed, and it is precisely this disappointment that really explains the character of these visions. For if what she saw were the result of her active imagination, the remembrance of this result would be accompanied by strong impressions of tense feeling. This feeling would be linked to the chain of delusion, and its highly agitated waves could not be calmed so suddenly. It is clear to us now that Theresa's imagination during the ecstatic visions is possessed by a higher power that makes use of it to cause a supernatural sympathetic love in her heart. Only a supernatural external power could perform the impossible and plunge the soul into this sea of pain. This power ceases to act after the ecstasy, and she is once more herself, left to her own reflections." [281]

This explanation of Therese Neumann's coldness the moment the visions are over is another example of the enthusiasm that prompts Archbishop Teodorowicz to theorize far beyond what is warranted by his evidence. Such is not the behaviour of

[280] *ibid.*, p. 466.
[281] *ibid.*, p. 465f.

those the Church has canonized. We think of Catherine of Siena, who wept for love when her ecstasy had ceased because she was no longer in the felt presence of her Beloved; we think of Teresa of Jesus, who wanted to die after ecstasy for the same reason. Were they, then, "linked to the chain of delusion" whose "highly agitated waves could not be calmed so suddenly" as Teodorowicz's hypothesis would imply? We have recalled only two of the better-known examples, but it is a common feature of true mystical ecstasy that it kindles and increases actual (as opposed to habitual) love so powerfully that its effects continue for some time. We know of no case—we write under correction—where the ecstatic returns to cold reflection immediately the ecstasy is over.[282] Even in the psychological order we may suppose that an experience as profound and moving as mystical union should produce what are called "after images," that is, reverberations which are projected into consciousness after the stimulus has ceased. Surely a vision is not like a film by which one is touched while seeing it but which is forgotten as soon as one has left the cinema?

On the other hand, we are told that "in Theresa's post-ecstatic state . . . we need only pay heed to the assertions that she makes in short, staccato fashion, and the operations of her soul are made clear . . . 'The Saviour is so good' is heard again and again during these moments . . . The pastor asks her if she loves the Saviour. She smiles. But this smile leaves in the minds of those who have once seen it an indelible impression . . . Other expressions show plainly and clearly that her soul is so strongly overcome with love of Christ that she shrinks from no sacrifice. 'I would give my life,' she answers the pastor, who says to her that if the Saviour is good, she should show that He is."[283] But this is not enough; the Archbishop has not demonstrated anything. These "ejaculations" only show that "she is once more herself, left to her own reflections;" they do not reveal the continuing influence of the ecstasy as it has been attested over and over again in the

[282] Cf. Alice Curtayne, *St. Catherine of Siena*, p. 57f., the passage beginning, "One little episode . . ."

[283] Teodorowicz, p. 467.

lives of the saints, who generally were unable to resume an ordinary conversation until some time after the ecstasy had ceased.

Here we may perhaps answer a possible objection. Is it not unfair, an opponent might say, and pressing a point, to compare Therese Neumann so insistently with the saints; are we not thereby making improper demands on her? The point here is that *we* are merely doing explicitly what all Therese's biographers have done implicitly. By assuming a supernatural origin of her experiences, they would seem to proclaim her to be in a state of heroic virtue and thus suggest that she may be placed one day among the saints; and one of the ways of verifying this is the very comparison questioned. This procedure can hardly be blamed as being unjust; for throughout this study it is the validity of this claim by Therese's advocates that we are examining. We impute nothing to Therese herself; for this is beyond our competence, just as it is beyond that of her admirers to declare the phenomena to be authentic. It would seem to be more consistent with the evidence available to regard the Konnersreuth occurrences with doubt. We hope to give more decisive reasons for this in our next chapter.

CHAPTER XV

The Interior Life (continued)

RECALLING FIRST to the reader's mind our introductory and closing comments of the previous chapter, we should now like to deal with two essentials of the spiritual life: penance and prayer. These are fundamental for any advance in holiness: every saint, regardless of the character of his sanctity, both advocated and practised penance; in order that a soul may become more conformed to the divine Image she must follow the example of her Master and tread her path to Calvary. Now, progress toward perfection always means advance in prayer. The soul whose prayer is more pure and loving is therefore also more pure and loving in herself.

Therese Neumann has occasionally been reproached for the absence of penance from her life, and Archbishop Teodorowicz defends her vigorously against this accusation. "But are hair-shirts and flagellations more indicative marks of mysticism than mortification and suffering in other ways? . . . With Therese Neumann the pains of the stigmata that she continuously has to suffer are equal to the severest voluntary mortifications. But above all, we need to ask whether her physical condition could stand scourgings and hair-shirts. Could her hands, marked with the wounds that cause her the most excruciating pain at the slightest touch, really guide the scourge, that needs a strong hand to hold it and to swing it effectively? I cannot imagine how Therese, with the large wound in her side, could wear a hair-shirt? What physical mortifications remain for her? Fasting? But she does not eat anything at all. Sleeping on a rough pallet? Yes; but she sleeps only about two hours every week. What, then, is left?" [284]

[284] Teodorowicz, p. 96.

This, of course, is all quite true. But Teodorowicz has not been thorough enough in his statement of the problem and its difficulties. We have little evidence that Therese, like other stigmatics, has ever had any ardent desire to undertake what voluntary penances are compatible with her health. Catherine of Siena is not known to have retreated to a more comfortable life after receiving the stigmata. And a discipline is not quite the formidable instrument the Archbishop makes it (it is not some kind of horror from the Inquisition) and can be used with little exertion. Indeed, it has always been necessary for confessors to restrain and caution their holy penitents against excessive self-punishment.

Moreover, the stigmata apparently do not prevent Therese from digging in the garden; according to an account from the *Katholisches Kirchenblatt* mentioned by Schimberg, this is an exercise she likes particularly.[285] Nor does a hair-shirt, in the form prescribed by Canon Law for women, cover the side, but only back and shoulders. Yet this type of penance is not suited for everyone, and Therese may well have been advised by her confessor not to adopt it. But, if this form of penance is excluded, should we not have more confidence in her holiness if we had evidence of other voluntary mortifications above the ordinary? It is impossible to state the exact amount of Therese's sleep, but it is well known that she spends considerable time in bed; and the objection has been made that this is a soft, Bavarian feather-bed which does not bespeak great penitential desires. "And if," replies Teodorowicz, "instead of the usual Bavarian bed, they saw the hard pallet of a Carthusian? 'There you have it'—he imagines visitors to reply—'everything for the sake of showing off.'"[286] Yet, in the case of the Saints, such penances have not provoked criticisms like those suggested.

There is, moreover, one voluntary mortification, prescribed by the Church's contemplative orders, within the power even of the most infirm, but which Teodorowicz neglects to include

[285] Schimberg, p. 26.
[286] Teodorowicz, p. 102.

among his list of possible ones: we mean the mortification of silence. It is the unanimous impression of visitors that Therese Neumann is particularly talkative: "*Elle fait des gestes bruyants et rit sans cesse à petits éclats. Elle aime causer*," writes Père Bruno.[287] And here is an extract from a letter of an American soldier who visited her during the occupation: "She asked me many questions and was so excited when I told her about my birds . . . We had to go back but she didn't want us to go. She wanted to talk about birds . . ."[288] We should note here that this form of mortification would be particularly meritorious because of her very inclination by temperament to conversation.

But there is a much more serious consideration than the absence of voluntary mortifications. So far as we can determine from all the sources, Therese apparently avoids as far as possible the involuntary ones that present themselves. For it is not specifically necessary that penance be deliberately sought: the lives of some men and women, in virtue of the circumstances in which God has seen fit to place them, are one continuous sequence of penance and renunciation, and the will may be thus purified by a loving submission in union with Christ crucified. In this connection we may profitably consider the electrically heated chair behind the high altar of the Konnersreuth parish church. Teodorowicz tells us that, "It was given to Theresa as a present. If we bear in mind that the generality of stigmatics, even as Theresa Neumann, in consequence of a great loss of blood and their ecstatic conditions, suffer from anæmia and chills, can we object to a heatable kneeling-bench, especially since the church is not heated? Does this priest [289] take offence because the confessional for the holy Curé d'Ars was heated?"[290]

Here the Archbishop is not dealing fairly with us; he clouds the issue with ambiguities. First of all, what Therese uses is not just a "kneeling-bench"; it is an elaborate construction in

---

[287] *Études Camélitaines*, Oct., 1936, p. 165.
[288] Schimberg, p. 5.
[289] An Hungarian who had objected to this.
[290] Teodorowicz, p. 94.

the shape of the priest's part of a confessional, furnished all over with soft cushions that are heated by means of a complicated network of electrical wiring (I examined it closely when I was in Konnersreuth). It was a present, it is true; and the suggestion usually offered is that she probably accepted it because Fr. Naber told her to do so. But we would submit, recalling the relationship between him and Therese discussed in a previous chapter, that if she had told him she was sure the Saviour did not like her to use such a luxury he would not have insisted. When I saw the many rheumatic old women who fill the Konnersreuth church, it was difficult not to remember another modern stigmatic, St. Gemma Galgani, who would give away her only warm skirt on a cold winter day to help a poor woman. As for the comparison with the Curé d'Ars—he accepted the little gift of a warmed footstool for his confessional, in which he spent sixteen to eighteen hours a day, in his old age, after a life of superhuman work and penance had broken his health. This slight alleviation of the sufferings of the great saint can scarcely be compared with the luxurious chair of which we speak. In addition, Therese only spends a very short time in the church, declaring that she is not a "*Betschwester*." [291]

In fact we are told that Therese likes the little pleasures of life, driving in cars, paying visits to her friends and relatives, chatting with those of her visitors whom she happens to like. All this is not incompatible with holiness; but it does seem opposed to the special mission of suffering which is claimed for Therese by herself and her biographers. We cannot endorse Teodorowicz's statement that, "If radio and the automobile had been available in the time of St. Theresa, we would not be surprised to find her in pleasant company in an automobile after nights of severe suffering." [292] It ought not to be necessary to remind an Archbishop that St. Theresa was a Carmelite nun bound to her extremely strict enclosure except when undertaking new foundations; nor is it a question, as he

[291] A derogatory term for a devout woman who spends much of her time in church.

[292] Teodorowicz, p. 98.

implies, of enjoying the beauties of God's creation, but of spending one's time in fruitless pursuits. Nor is it very probable that modern Carmelites indulge in listening to the wireless or driving about in cars " in pleasant company." From a presupposition of a redemptive mission of suffering, certain results ought logicaly to follow; and it would not be expected that participating in the superfluities of modern civilization is one of them.

Therese is reported as having once said to Dr. Gerlich: " You know, doctor, when a person has to undergo as much as I do and has the vocation to listen to so many people's sufferings and troubles, he is grateful and glad to laugh at some harmless joke. . . . Today it helps me a great deal and refreshes me when I can talk to you about light things." [293] Certainly even the greatest mystic needs recreation from time to time. St. Teresa speaks of this in many places. But we find that in the life of Therese Neumann these recreations are given a surprisingly large share of her time. It is the discrepancy here, between the vocation of suffering and her ordinary life, that is puzzling, not the fact that such careless activities are present. This desire for the natural pleasures of life, combined with the absence of voluntary mortification and the avoidance of humiliations discussed in the last chapter, shows quite plainly that, except for the complex of stigmatization and expiatory sufferings—considered by Poray-Madeyski, Fr. Thornton and others to be the manifestations of a hysterical neurosis—mortification is not the dominant note in Therese's spiritual life. This circumstance would make the assertions of her biographers on her behalf seem somewhat incautious.

Another unusual feature is Therese's attitude to the sufferings of Our Lord. According to Tanquerey, " The stigmata are not met with except in persons who *practise the most heroic virtues* and possess a special love for the Cross." [294] Despite the conclusions at which we arrived in the last chapter, perhaps the presence of the stigmata may be accounted for by an

[293] *ibid.*, p. 58.
[294] Tanquerey, *The Spiritual Life*, Eng. trans., 2nd ed., no. 1524.5; his italics.

ardent devotion to the Passion in accordance with a statement
from the *Études Carmélitaines* which reads: "If one notices
. . . after the stigmatization, a greater scorn for the
world . . . a more generous love of Jesus Crucified and of the
sufferings that assimilate us to Him, a progress in the contemplation of the depths of the Passion and the abasement of
Jesus . . . one has the proof that the stigmatization is an
authentic mystical fact." [295]

Now, the strange fact is that outside the trances Therese
evinces extremely little devotion to the Passion of Christ. This
is not to say that it is not present, but certain characteristics
make it necessary to consider this point. We have already
noted her behaviour immediately after the visions have ceased.
Teodorowicz has examined this question particularly in order
to refute the theory of unbelievers that stigmatization is produced by the concentration of the mind on the sufferings of
Christ. "If a strong concentration of the mind on the sufferings of Christ would suffice to explain the appearance of the
stigmata, precisely this sort of concentration was lacking in the
interior life of Theresa during her long illness. I have made
exact inquiry on this point of Theresa herself and asked her
various questions without her knowing my purpose. The result
was that I ascertained she did not have any particular devotion
to the Passion before the stigmatization and made absolutely no
meditation on the sufferings of Christ." [296] The question
immediately arises: if no devotion to the Passion before, then
perhaps after? "Meditation on the sufferings of Our Lord . . .
has become almost a physical impossibility at the present time.
I was much astonished and her words sounded like a revelation
to me when, in answer to my question whether outside the
ecstasy she liked to meditate on the sufferings of Christ, she
answered that she did not care to meditate on them at all.
This subject affects her physically most severely and therefore
she never touches upon it in meditation. At that time I was
attending a mission that was being given by the Capuchins at
Konnersreuth. She gave me a new example that brightly

[295] *Études Carm.*, Garrigou-Lagrange and Lavaud, Oct., 1936, p. 199.
[296] Teodorowicz, p. 292.

illumined what has already been said of her. She was making the mission and attending the devotions in the church. 'I reached the church,' she told me, 'just when they were praying the sorrowful mysteries of the rosary . . . It was altogether impossible for me to take any further part in the exercises. In spite of the commotion that I caused, I had to leave the church at once during the prayers.' That is the spiritual condition in which she now finds herself." [297]

This account is illuminating in more ways than one, as even the most cursory reading will show. The archbishop is concerned with unbelievers who would accuse Therese of producing her trances, etc., by autosuggestion. But while trying to avoid the Scylla of the unbelievers, he falls into the Charybdis of the mystical theologians [298] who consider the stigmata without an intense devotion to the Passion an impossibility. Therese's conduct while the sorrowful mysteries were being said is quite incomprehensible. She has told us that her mission in life is suffering, that this is a means of saving souls superior even to her former desire, the missionary vocation; now it seems that meditation on the sufferings of Our Lord causes her physical pain, " and therefore she never touches upon it in meditation." Are we to conclude, as this indicates, that Therese only meditates on the pleasing events in Our Lord's life, because thus she avoids suffering? This appears improbable; for all Our Lord's actions and words point to Calvary as the cause and climax of the Incarnation. Even the glories of the Resurrection and Ascension are unintelligible without the bitter sufferings of the Cross. Christ's redeeming Passion is the central fact of the Gospels; unless it be also the centre of our prayer, our spiritual life lacks its foundation.

There remains this: if Therese does not like to occupy herself with the Passion of Our Lord in her prayer outside the Friday trances, what is her life of prayer in her ordinary state? Here again, our study must necessarily be incomplete owing to lack of material. The most definite statement we could find is that

[297] *ibid.*, p. 295.

[298] We have already indicated that his terminology is not the accepted one.

of Fr. Naber, who says that, "Theresa is always in the state of mystical quiet . . . . No deliberation, no analysis, no discussion, but perseverance in a continuous silent state of love; that is the main principle of her prayer." [299]

This statement needs clarification. As it is the only one which, as I have just said, could be found in the literature accessible to me, I have to interpret it more closely than I would have done otherwise; but I think the conclusions I shall draw are consonant with the whole tenor of her spiritual life as it appears in these pages. Language here is an unfortunate barrier; but since it is the only human mode of communication, one would prefer those words which have a certain degree of intelligibility in these matters. Here are a few of the difficulties:

First, what is meant by "the state of mystical quiet"? Is it the Prayer of Quiet described by St. Teresa; and if so, what are we to understand by the word "always"? It may mean one of two things: either that Therese Neumann's prayer is habitually the Prayer of Quiet, as opposed to any other form of prayer; or that always, whatever her occupation of the moment, whether in formal prayer or out of it, she is in the state of "mystical quiet"; that is to say that the Prayer of Quiet continues uninterruptedly. If the Prayer of Quiet is meant, both these answers would be unsatisfactory. For St. Teresa says that this prayer is only a transitional stage—it is a Prelude to the Prayer of Union and the Prayer of Ecstasy. She writes: "If God gives a soul such pledges (viz., the Prayer of Quiet) it is a sign that He has great things in store for it. It will be its own fault if it does not make great progress." [300] But Therese Neumann is presumed to have ecstatic prayer habitually, at least during the Friday trances. Now ecstatics, when not actually in ecstasy, would have a prayer higher than the Prayer of Quiet which, after all, is only the very first step in mystical prayer properly so called; they would revert to complete union. It is therefore not likely that Therese's prayer outside the Friday trances would be habitually only the Prayer

[299] Teodorowicz, p. 162.
[300] *Way of Perfection*, Chapter 31 (Allison Peers, II, p. 133).

of Quiet. On the other hand, it seems equally unlikely that, outside her actual prayer, she should constantly be in a state of "mystical quiet." For St. Teresa says: "When this quiet is felt in a high degree and lasts for a long time . . . sometimes it goes on for a day, or for two days . . . ." [301] From this we infer that it is not a state in which one can "always" be.

But it may be that Fr. Naber, in speaking of "mystical quiet," does not mean the same as St. Teresa's Prayer of Quiet. For Therese Neumann is opposed to all such categories of prayer. "Therese, with all the vivacity of her temperament, manifested her aversion against all sorts of classification and gradation in this matter: This building of little heaps, this strict gradation of degrees of perfection I cannot bear at all." [302] No doubt this type of classification can sometimes be exaggerated; it is nonetheless true that the gradations of prayer have been accepted by the Church from very early times. We need only mention the seventh-century Greek writer, St. John Climacus, with his *Scala Paradisi* and its thirty divisions; or St. Teresa's *Mansions*, which has become the generally accepted classification of the spiritual life in the Church of today.

What, then, is this "mystical quiet"? Taken together with Therese's opposition to the recitation of the Breviary, to gradations of the spiritual life, to occupation with the Passion outside her trances, one is inclined to suspect a certain resemblance to the prayer of the Quietists (to whom we have referred before), who strove as much as possible always to be in such a "continuous silent state of love." This is the heresy of inaction which, in the guise of simplicity and abandonment, would deny to creatures their efficacy as secondary causes. A more positive description of Therese's prayer would have been more encouraging; the very fact that it is so indefinite disposes one to doubt. And Archbishop Teodorowicz's explanation of this state of prayer *and* the absence of devotion to the Passion, so fanciful and inexact, does little to dissolve doubt.

[301] *ibid.,* p. 128f.
[302] Lavaud, *Études Carm.,* April, 1933, p. 79; cited by Poray-Madeyski, p. 93.

"Her natural (*sic*) moral relations to Christ," he writes, "do not need a special sinking into the Passion of Christ. She shows as little particular devotion to the martyred Saviour as she did before, even though in the ecstasies she lives through His Passion, because the core of her mystical relation to Christ is not the experiencing and the contemplation of Christ's suffering and death, but that state of mystical silence." [303] Is this, after all, the real meaning of the saints when they spoke of being "ravished by love"? St. Teresa, in the Sixth Mansion of her *Interior Castle* which deals with ecstasy, writes: "Some souls also imagine that they cannot dwell upon the Passion. . . . I cannot conceive what they are thinking of; for though angelic spirits, freed from everything corporeal, may remain permanently enkindled in love, this is not possible for those of us who live in this mortal body. . . ." [304] In another place she says: "There will be many souls who derive greater benefits from other meditations than from that of the Sacred Passion . . . they derive great comfort and benefit from considering the power and greatness of God in the creatures. . . . This is an admirable procedure, provided one does not fail to meditate often upon the Passion and the Life of Christ, which are, and always have been, the source of everything that is good." [305]

Thus, Therese Neumann's refusal to concern herself with the Passion, together with this peculiar and undefined "state of mystical silence" which, insofar as can be determined from Fr. Naber and Archbishop Teodorowicz, knows no vicissitudes, presses this conclusion upon us: this state of prayer is neither mystical nor pre-mystical, but akin to the prayer of the Quietists. Dom Aloys Mager writes in connection with Teodorowicz's book: "But it is not proved that she enjoys infused contemplation" (this after all is the most important thing). "Another demonstration would be indispensable." [306] We are left with uncertainty; and until more material is forthcoming, this can be the only consistent and truthful attitude.

[303] Teodorowicz, p. 163.
[304] *Interior Castle*, VI, 7 (II, 304f).
[305] *Life*, 13 (I, p. 79).
[306] *Études Carm.*, Oct., 1936, p. 155.

Conclusion

WE HAVE now concluded the body of this study, in which we have formally examined various aspects of the occurrences at Konnersreuth in the light of certain principles of the teaching Church and of the experiences of the saints as they have been transmitted to us. To sum up our findings: a supernatural origin of the phenomena exhibited by Therese Neumann is not *necessarily* demanded by the evidence at our disposal which, admittedly, is not as complete, in many respects, as one might desire. Rather must we affirm at this point that the greatest caution and circumspection ought to be exercised by anyone who approaches this case with the intention of a serious investigation; for even if the stigmata and the other events be not considered mystical but charismatic gifts, the fact that they have appeared in connection with illnesses certified by the examining doctors as hysterical in nature and do not correspond with similar experiences in the history of the Church's saints would still justify a reasonable doubt.

In this concluding chapter we should like to consider two objections that have been made to us and have not been dealt with in the preceding pages. These objections are: (1) that Therese Neumann has remained the simple peasant girl she has always been; (2) that conversions have actually been effected through her.

The first is not a particularly difficult one. It is certainly true that Therese still lives the life of a Bavarian peasant woman in her native village; essentially she has not changed her mode of life, her habits and customs, and her conduct is much as it has always been. But it must be pointed out that if this be a proof of her supernatural graces, then the circumstance that St. Catherine of Siena went out into the world, even to the Papal court of Avignon, and that she acquired a wide knowledge of many things and connections with a vast number of people, far exceeding the normal possibilities of her humble origin—then all this, I say, could be held to disprove that her graces were supernatural. In fact, this accusation was made in her lifetime, just as similar reasons were brought against St. Teresa of Jesus. But as little as the activities of these saints can be adduced against them, as little reason is there for considering Therese Neumann's simple village life proof of the supernatural character of the phenomena of Konnersreuth. The only conclusion that can validly be drawn from this fact is that she has sufficient good sense to realize that she would be very ill-advised if she attempted to lead another life entirely unsuited to her nature and upbringing. For what possibilities would be open to her? "'Business enterprises could have been found,' says Cardinal Faulhaber, 'that would have rebuilt the Neumann house into a theatre. Millions would have been paid if Theresa in her suffering condition would have been filmed and been shown in the motion picture houses of Europe.' But the honourable Mr. Neumann rejected this bid." [307]

But this would merely justify one or both of two possible inferences: (1) that the Neumanns are God-fearing, sensible people, to whom sudden fabulous riches are no temptation; (2) that they are probably quite aware that as soon as Therese's trances were converted into a commercial enterprise, this would be the end of them as far as the Church was concerned. It seems most probable that, confronted with the choice between their daughter's reputation for sanctity and the offer of Mammon, they would quite naturally choose the former. It is important to remember that the prestige and dignity they hold are maintained not only by the startling nature of their daughter's experiences, but perhaps primarily by the note of holiness attributed to them by the faithful the world over. If the latter went, as it most certainly would if

[307] Cited by Teodorowicz, p. 50.

Konnersreuth were capitalized commercially, so would their present position.

In fact, apart from altogether endangering her reputation by accepting a film offer, no other alternative to the life she is leading presents itself. It must surely be obvious to her that in any place other than Konnersreuth, where she is surrounded by the care and affection of her family and the guidance of Fr. Naber, she would be like a fish out of water; for she has had no training for any other kind of life. Besides, she has everything she wants in Konnersreuth. Admirers from every part of the world come to visit her, she is respected and venerated, and she has her parents and Fr. Naber to shield her from those she does not wish to see. What could she possibly gain by leaving this sphere that suits her so perfectly? Nothing could be better fitted to her needs and personality.

The second objection is worthy of more serious consideration, since there have been conversions in Konnersreuth. Perhaps the most famous is that of Gerlich, a former Calvinist, who received the gift of faith at Konnersreuth. Schimberg, Therese's latest biographer, mentions a Counsellor Schondorf and a Dr. Becker among converts from Protestantism, and a Dr. Karpeles and Bruno Rothschild from Judaism.[308] Doubtless there have been many more; but what must be noted is the absence of conversions in great numbers. There is nothing resembling the mass conversions effected by such saints as Francis de Sales, Catherine of Siena, or the Curé d'Ars. There is no crowded confessional in the church at Konnersreuth, no mass return of heretics and apostates to the faith, nor have any such claims ever been made by even the most ardent devotees. Now, large numbers of conversions need not necessarily follow the phenomena we are examining; but in this case their absence is striking because of one particular fact. Therese has said: "All that (viz., her graces) is not for me; it is for others. I myself, with all these gifts, can be damned."[309] If this is true, if all these graces—the stigmata, clairvoyance, inedia, etc.—are only for others, then surely we

[308] Schimberg, p. 230.
[309] Teodorowicz, p. 167.

must logically expect them to produce tremendous fruits; among the thousands of visitors coming to Konnersreuth every year there should be hundreds of conversions. When I was in Regensburg in the summer of 1948, after there had been, according to the estimate of Schimberg, at least 12,000 American soldiers at Konnersreuth,[310] I asked the Vicar General of the diocese whether there had been many conversions amongst the Americans. His reply was: " Not that I know of." What actually did happen was that, " She told them (the American soldiers) she was going into the other room to get a holy picture for each soldier, and that she would be glad to autograph the picture." [311] " Up to April of this year (1946)," Schimberg tells us, " Therese Neumann had given more than 10,000 little holy pictures to as many American visitors." [312] May we not suppose that if these phenomena were truly graces given for others, the influx of thousands of American troops should have produced innumerable conversions? And would it not have been more satisfying to find Fr. Naber busy in the confessional rather than Therese autographing holy pictures?

But can it not be argued that the very fact of any conversions at all proves the phenomena to be supernatural? We think not. The grace of God works in strange ways, and His Love and omnipotence make use of many means—even of plays like Oberammergau and of films in order to change men's hearts. There have been many devout, though very imperfect Christians, who have been responsible for many conversions: remember Léon Bloy who had the distinction of bringing into the Church Jacques and Raissa Maritain, as well as many others.

There is a rather famous case that will help to illustrate our point. We refer to Palma Matarrelli, of Oria, mentioned before. According to Fr. Thurston,[313] Pope Pius IX judged her very severely, going even so far as to call her activities " the

[310] Schimberg, p. 10.
[311] *ibid.*, p. 8.
[312] *ibid.*, p. 11.
[313] *The Month,* Oct., 1919, p. 299.

work of the devil." Yet, says Fr. Thurston, "there is evidence that Palma sometimes influenced souls for good. For example, a friend writes to me: There was a married woman, a cousin of mine, living a very frivolous and worldly life in Paris. She went to see Palma as a new excitement, not with serious purpose. Palma knew all about her and had a message for her from Our Lord. She was to return to Paris and seek a certain Father, whose name I forgot, and make a general confession in preparation for death, for she was not to live long. While with Palma, my cousin saw the Sacred Host come miraculously and enter Palma's mouth. Overwhelmed with astonishment and fear, she was at once converted. Returning to Paris, she did as Palma had desired and lived a most holy life for a few weeks or months, and then died a very edifying death. . . . I repeat this statement as I received it, only adding that I am fully assured of the good faith of the writer, who has long been known to me personally and by repute for more than thirty years." [314]

We see, then, that God in His infinite mercy may sometimes use the faith of those who come into contact with persons like Palma d'Oria in order to give them graces; but so far as we know, these incidents remain comparatively few; they are out of proportion to the magnitude of the phenomena which, if genuinely supernatural and bestowed for the benefit of others, should produce conversions by the thousand. But as has been said before, even her most devoted admirers have never been able to produce evidence for more than a few cases.

There is one last objection that is sometimes put forward against a natural explanation of the phenomena, namely, that through Konnersreuth Almighty God is recalling to an apostate world the Passion of His Son. This may quite well be true: one cannot penetrate the divine Mind; but there have been cases of stigmatization from the time of St. Francis to his saintly son, the Capuchin Padre Pio, at the present day—Therese Neumann is only one of hundreds. If this truly should be her particular mission—an apostolate of pain and the Cross—two

[314] *ibid.*, pp. 300ff.

conditions might be expected to be fulfilled: (1) evident sanctity in the person entrusted with this apostolate, so that all possibility of justified scandal (as contrasted with *scandalum pharisaicum*) would be excluded; (2) conversions on a grand scale, and very probably miracles would be required as credentials. That these are not present at Konnersreuth is certainly no condemnation of Therese Neumann; there are few people who could make such claims. But the difference in the present instance is that certain things have been proclaimed which would demand more for proof of their validity than the sensational events and unsubstantiated pious legends of Konnersreuth.

We have indicated several times in the course of this study that it is not within our competence to make a conclusive decision on the phenomena exhibited by Therese Neumann. However, by this time our position should be quite clear, and so long as the Church has not expressed a judgment in a different sense, it cannot be dismissed arbitrarily by merely pointing to the presence of her stigmata and visions. We must reply: the evidence is there, suggestive indications are there, but many things that ought to be there are not. Here is the crux of the whole matter: it is in the interests of true mysticism to apply its principles to phenomena popularly called "mystical" and to guard against confusing all manner of strange psychological states—which, by the way, may even appear, and actually have appeared, in the lives of genuine mystics—with what is truly mystical: the union of a perfectly humble and loving soul with God. From this union may indeed arise many strange phenomena, and it is these that can be counterfeited, whether by hysteria and its attendant psychological conditions or by the devil. St. John of the Cross knew this well, which is precisely the reason why he inveighed so relentlessly against putting one's trust in such things. In themselves, in the spiritual order, they are of little importance; all their value arises from the underlying union with God that they serve to express—like a banknote, the paper and pictures of which are worthless if there are no assets supporting the currency.

Alas, since men live by their senses, they are easily led to judge by the pictures, by that which *might* represent holiness, without asking if the fundamental reality is present, too. But in the interests of Truth and the Church, phenomena, however striking, ought to be examined and investigated. There is no danger to our faith in this. On the contrary, for as the Apostle says, Faith is "the evidence of things that appear not." But "phenomena," according to the etymology of the term, are the things that appear; they may sometimes be given in order to strengthen our faith, but it is a most dangerous proceeding to put our trust in them. Our Lord says: Blessed are they that have not seen and have believed; and by His words we must live.

The Stigmatic of Hamburg

A FTER this book had been finished there was brought to our notice an extraordinary case of "stigmatization" which was given great publicity in the German papers at the end of July, 1949. We give a short account of it from these reports without, however, taking any responsibility for the accuracy of the facts, which we have not been able to investigate.

According to the newspaper reports, the stigmatized person is a well-to-do Protestant timber merchant, Arthur Otto M., who lives at Berne, a suburb of Hamburg. He was born in the Alsatian town of Hagenau in 1902, but has been living in or near Hamburg since 1906. In May, 1928, he had a car accident, after which he experienced certain strange phenomena, the exact character of which is not specified in the newspaper articles. They became more prominent after 1935, and it is pointed out that in Therese Neumann's case, too, the stigmata appeared just seven years after the accident of the fire. From 1935 the wounds of the Crown of Thorns appeared on Herr M.'s head, at first only three or four times a year, later more frequently. Afterwards the other stigmata developed on his hands, feet and side; they appear about every four or six weeks. In 1943 he was flung down a high staircase by the draft caused by the explosion of an h.e. bomb during an air raid. As a consequence, a distinct cross appeared on his forehead. It is interesting to note that he was never called up for military service owing to his weak heart and a defect in his spine.

"The phenomenon," writes Professor Georg Anschuetz in the *Nord-West-Illustrierte* of 23rd July, 1949, "which out of its ordinary periodical rhythm appears only under stress of great excitement, is preceded by strong pressure on both sides of the head, together with intense headache. 'I feel like having lead in my head,' he said in conversation. The opening of the stigmata takes place a few minutes later and is always marked by a distinct sensation of relief. Though there can be no question of particular psychical disturbances, this state is accompanied by a series of noteworthy experiences. Sometimes a black wall appears before his eyes. The senses of hearing and seeing, too, are occasionally completely put out of action. Immediately before the wounds open a religious vision appears: from the distance the Saviour approaches him, dressed in a flowing blue garment; he holds a book in his hands and speaks kind and consoling words to him. Then He slowly disappears into the infinite. With this the pressure ceases. . . ."

There are other interesting phenomena. "Herr M.," continues Professor Anschuetz, "often no longer feels to be himself. Sometimes his ego splits to such an extent that he sees himself a whole day beside or opposite himself, though in the same clothes. The outlines of objects such as tables and chairs appear double. Some objects, and even men, are transparent . . . Herr M. also has the gift of a certain fore-knowledge. He often knows with absolute certainty beforehand of letters which are going to arrive and of visitors who will come. He suffers much not only from the stigmata but also from these phenomena. For many years he has had the ardent desire to be freed from them."

He also no longer sleeps, but only rests, propped up on pillows. His weight has dropped to about half of what it was before the phenomena appeared, and his capacity of work has diminished considerably.

We have said before that Herr M. is a Protestant—but he is that only in name. He does not go to church and takes little interest in religion, though he has a certain vague veneration for the Deity, as is often the case with educated Germans professing no particular religious faith. Nor seems the "stigmatization" to have had any effect on his inner life, since his only desire is to be freed from these strange phenomena.

It is not within our competence to give an explanation of this remarkable case. However, what seems certain is that there must be some Catholic influence somewhere in order to account for the phenomena; else the case would be nothing less than a miracle: the impression of the stigmata without any possibility of a natural explanation. We know nothing of Herr M.'s upbringing, influences, the books he has read, etc., but there seems at least one strong possibility of a psychological influence, suggested by a comparison of dates. The case of Therese Neumann was eagerly discussed throughout both Catholic and Protestant Germany just before Herr M. had his car accident (we remember that the publicity began in 1926 and reached its peak after the favourable result of the investigation of her inedia in July, 1927). Hence, Herr M. must have known about it and probably interested himself in it shortly before this accident in 1928, after which the first strange phenomena began to appear, just as Therese's did after the accident of the fire. The connecting link with Catholicism would then be found in her.

There is, however, a significant difference between the Catholic and the Protestant stigmatic, which seems to us at least an indication of the non-supernatural origin of the phenomena. For whereas the visions of the former take the elaborate form suggested by Catholic art and ritual, those of Herr M. are very simple. There are no visions of the Passion, with the details of which he is perhaps not familiar, seeing that one of the newspaper articles says that his Bible lies in an old box in an attic of the house and is never opened. To him Christ appears as He is often represented on Protestant pictures, for example on those by Uhde, as a gentle-looking man in a long, wide garment. Obviously, there is nothing else for him on which to feed his imagination, whether consciously or subconsciously. It was the same with Mollie Fancher, whose trance visions were confined to the souls of the departed and similar rather colourless subjects.

On the other hand, the accompanying phenomena, such as clairvoyance and a certain knowledge of future events, are present in the Protestant as well as in the Catholic stigmatist; with the difference that in the case of the former their development was not encouraged; inability to sleep, which seems a common feature of most stigmatics, is characteristic also of Herr M.; only the lack of food (the most notable trait of Mollie

Fancher) is not mentioned in the reports that have come to my knowledge.

It would seem, then, that however much our sensibilities and feelings may revolt against it (and I frankly admit that my own do) there is such a thing as purely neurotic (for want of a better name) stigmatization, completely divorced from the supernatural. How else is it to be explained that an unbelieving Protestant bears all the bloodmarks of the Passion in his body without any other effect on him than annoyance and the eager desire to get rid of them?

So far medical experts as well as psychologists are confronted with a riddle; they can neither free the unfortunate man from what he himself regards as a disease that hinders his work, nor can they explain in what exactly it consists. From the theological point of view it may be said that a supernatural intervention is so improbable that it can be ruled out unless (which seems unlikely) the case should have some far-reaching religious effects in the future.

Some people may be troubled by these phenomena and wonder why God allows all the external signs of stigmatization to appear in an unbeliever. The "Why does God allow" question is very old, and the classic answer is that given by the inspired prophet: "For my thoughts are not your thoughts: nor your ways my ways, saith the Lord. For as the heavens are exalted above the earth, so are my ways exalted above your ways, and my thoughts above your thoughts." [1]

Yet a case like this of the stigmatized Protestant merchant seems to us a most convincing proof of the truth of the teaching of the Mystical Doctor of the Church: beware of strange phenomena, live by faith. "For if a man make much account of these miracles," [2] writes St. John of the Cross, "he ceases to lean upon the substantial practice of faith which is an obscure habit; and thus, where signs and witnesses abound, there is less merit in believing . . . Because of their joy in these works, men commonly fall into vainglory or some other vanity. For even their joy in these wonders, when it is not . . . purely in God and for God, is vanity." [3]

[1] Isai. 55:8-9.
[2] The word here used in a loose sense, like marvel, wonder.
[3] *Complete Works*, I, p. 305f.

A NOTE ON THE TYPE

IN WHICH THIS BOOK WAS SET

This book is set in Caledonia, a Linotype face created in 1939 by W. A. Dwiggins, which is by far one of the best book types created in the last 50 years. It has a simple, hard-working, feet-on-the-ground quality and can be classed as a modern type face with excellent color and good readability. The designer claims Caledonia was created by putting a little of each of Scotch Roman, Bulmer, Baskerville and Bodoni together and producing a lively crisp-like book type. This book was composed and printed by the York Composition Company of York, Pa., and bound by Moore and Company of Baltimore. The typography and design of this book were by Howard N. King.